the cinema was becoming increasingly a part of social life of the working classes and should be financially and personally supported by anyone seeking to uplift the masses."

Gorleston and Great Yarmouth, too, were destined to have new, luxurious picture houses delivered by F H Cooper. He opened Filmland in Gorleston in 1913, which was very popular and known locally as the "Gorleston Cosy" because it was heated and featured leather padded seats.

Frederick continued building and buying picture houses around the region, including the ambitious Regent in Great Yarmouth, which opened in 1914. By 1916, he had an impressive chain of electric theatres, collectively known as East Counties Electric Theatres Limited.

As his business flourished and his chain of cinemas spread across the county, he sought a bigger property from which to work and live. In 1917, he bought the Banks of the Yare estate in Brundall. It was ideally placed on the eastern side of Norwich with links to Great Yarmouth and the rest of East Anglia. The large estate covered 300 acres and had previously been owned by Dr Michael Beverley, a local physician.

Dr Beverley had developed a beautiful and exotic garden estate that led down to Brundall Mere. The estate featured rare plants and trees, brought back from his trips abroad. AH Patterson in his article *An Ideal River Excursion* described it thus: "What a wealth of oaks, weeping ashes, and elms, and coniferous trees of many sorts... what walks, glades, arbours and leafy nooks

THE REFRESHMENT ROOM, BRUNDALL GARDENS

lead up from the lily-smothered lake to the hill-top, where miles of landscape hold the onlooker enraptured."

Initially, Frederick and his family lived in a Log House on the estate built by Dr Beverley. The house burnt down in 1919 and Frederick constructed a new residence called Redclyffe House. The house was constructed by the same architects and builders he had used to build his extravagant picture houses. Many of the rooms at Redclyffe featured similarly ornate plaster mouldings. The Coopers entertained lavishly at Redclyffe, where guests included the celebrated writer and director Edgar Wallace, who wrote the novel on which *King Kong* was based.

Ever the entrepreneur, Frederick saw the opportunity of opening the garden up to the public. He designed a circular walk around the estate and even persuaded the North London Eastern Railway to build a halt on the line at Brundall, resulting in the Brundall Gardens station that exists to this day.

The enterprise developed considerably over the years, with Frederick later establishing the Brundall Gardens Steamship Company, which ran day trips to Great Yarmouth. He also developed a playground, tennis courts and a small museum filled with Roman artefacts drawn from the dock. As the number of visitors grew, Frederick also built The Riverside Hotel and a large restaurant on the banks of the river.

Soon Brundall Gardens had been transformed into a large holiday resort teeming with visitors during the summer months. In the summer of 1922, a staggering 60,000 people visited the resort. New rentable cottages were built and the resort was promoted as the "Switzerland of the Broads" due to its stunning scenery and gardens.

As well as the estate and his cinemas, Frederick was also concerned with the conditions of those involved in film-making and distribution. In 1918, he formed the Eastern Counties branch of the Cinematograph Exhibitors' Association (CEA).

Frederick and his associates attended the Conference of Motion Picture Theatre Owners of America in Milwaukee. They also met Charlie Chaplin on the set of *The Gold Rush*, Mary Pickford at Fox Studios and toured the sets of Universal Studios. On their return, the delegates attended the CEA conference and lobbied for measures to address the domination of American films in Britain.

Eventually, in 1927, the Cinematograph Films Act was established compelling every proprietor to include a quota of British films. The quotas were introduced by degrees, from 7.5% to 20% over the next 10 years. Largely because of Frederick's support of the British film industry, he was elected Vice-President of the CEA

❝Ever the entrepreneur, Frederick saw the opportunity of opening the garden up to the public. He designed a circular walk around the estate and even persuaded the North London Eastern Railway to build a halt on the line at Brundall, resulting in the Brundall Gardens station that exists to this day.❞

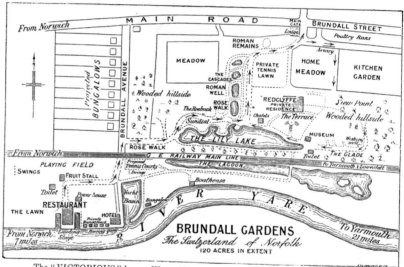

The "VICTORIOUS" leaves West side of Southtown Bridge every morning (except Saturdays and Sundays) at 10 o'clock, returning at 6.30 p m.
42 miles for 3/- - " " " " - And 6d. for the Gardens.

in 1928 and became President in 1929. In June of 1929, he travelled to Paris and lead England's delegation at the European Cinema Congress. On the occasion he spoke about the arrival of the "talkies". He could see the difficulties that could occur with language when each country made its own talking films. He thought the issues could be overcome if a picture was synchronised in the language of the exhibiting nation. In this, he foresaw "dubbing".

He warned exhibitors about entering into contracts for hiring or buying early sound equipment, which subsequently became "a pig in a poke", in other words no longer fit for purpose.

Later that year, the CEA held their annual conference in Great Yarmouth. On one day

Welcome to
Norfolk at the Pictures

ACKNOWLEDGEMENTS

PROJECT CO-ORDINATOR	MARC ATKINSON
EDITOR	ANNA WOOD
WRITERS & CONTRIBUTORS	MICHAEL ARMSTRONG
	MARC ATKINSON
	BASIL ABBOTT
	COLIN ALDIS
	CHARLES BARR
	MELLISSA BEEKEN
	DENIS BISHOP
	ANNA BLAGROVE
	TONY BRITTEN
	DAVID CLEVELAND
	PETER COSSEY
	LUCY COWBURN
	CHARLOTTE DAY
	MARTIN FIGURA
	HANNAH GARRARD
	RONALD GREEN
	SIR JOHN HURT
	MIKE HUTCHINSON
	HELEN IVORY
	JOHN JARVIS
	VALERIE JORDAN
	GUY MARTIN
	ANDREW McDONNELL
	SILVIA ROSE
	DAVID STANDEN
	REBECCA STEEL
	NICK STONE
	LEO TEMPLE
	BRYAN WATERS
	JULIA WEBB
	TREVOR WICKS
DESIGNED & PUBLISHED BY	ARCHANT/EDP
PRODUCED BY	CINEMA PLUS AND ARCHANT MEDIA
FUNDED BY	THE HERITAGE LOTTERY FUND
PICTURES COURTESY OF	NORFOLK COUNTY COUNCIL
	PICTURE NORFOLK
	ARCHANT/EASTERN DAILY PRESS
	THE RONALD GRANT ARCHIVE
	THE GEORGE PLUNKETT COLLECTION

I am delighted to introduce this special commemorative magazine produced by Cinema Plus, the film education charity at Cinema City. This unique magazine collects together some of the memories, stories and pictures gathered through the Heritage Lottery Funded project Norfolk at the Pictures. The magazine also looks at the films screened in local cinemas and the popularity of the region for filmmakers today.

As I discuss later in relation to my own memories, most people clearly recall their first visits to the cinema and I hope you enjoy finding out more about the rich history of cinema-going in Norfolk through the recollections of staff, enthusiasts and cinemagoers from across this wonderful county.

Sir John Hurt, patron of Cinema City

This magazine has been made possible through a generous grant from the Heritage Lottery Fund and the hard work of volunteers and contributors from across Norfolk. We welcome your feedback on the magazine. To contact us, find out more about the Norfolk at the Pictures project or submit your own cinema memories visit **norfolkatthepictures.org.uk**

ALBROW & SONS LTD

FAMILY JEWELLERS

Victorian opal and diamond pendant

Diamond solitaire 2.57ct certificated G/VS

Certificated finest AAA grade Hanadama cultured pearls

Edwardian emerald and diamond earrings

10 ALL SAINTS GREEN • NORWICH • NORFOLK • NR1 3NA • 01603 622569

OPPOSITE JOHN LEWIS

THE NATIONAL
ASSOCIATION
OF GOLDSMITHS

"Representing retail jewellers since 1894"

CHARLIE CHAPLIN STUDIOS' SET FOR 'GOLD RUSH'. F.H.C. AND CHARLIE CHAPLIN (FIRST AND THIRD RIGHT)

CHAPLIN AND BOB HOPE ON THE 'GOLD RUSH' SET

the entire conference of exhibitors from all over England travelled to Brundall, where they were entertained with tea and talks in a marquee on the lawns of the famous gardens.

Frederick was also instrumental in campaigning for cinemas to be opened on Sundays and continued to speak against the entertainment tax. Personally, however, he suffered from ill-health. He had been diagnosed as a diabetic in 1928 and in 1930 he embarked upon some new ventures which were to backfire. He bought the Theatre Royal in Great Yarmouth and the derelict Marina Theatre in Lowestoft to convert them for live entertainment and film shows with sound.

A considerable investment was involved with huge overdrafts but much of the capital was Frederick's own. The economic crisis provoked by the Great Depression forced the banks to foreclose on borrowings and Frederick was faced with redeeming his significant loans. He refused to go bankrupt, attempting to pay off his debts by using some of his wife's money and renting out the estate at Brundall.

His efforts were to no avail and after losing all his money, he suffered a stroke and the Cooper family moved - first to London to stay with relatives and then to Gloucestershire.

In 1936, the Brundall estate was sold and Fredrick died a few years later in 1939 at the age of 72. Sadly, his life had seemingly come full circle, having started with little and ending in the same way. In life, however, he rose to a national level of distinction in the cinema trade and his passion and hard-work still influence the way in which we watch films today.

With thanks to Caroline Seville, Stephen Peart and Gerald Hawkins.

THE PICTURE DESTINED TO STARTLE THE WORLD!

KING KONG

with
FAY WRAY · ROB'T ARMSTRONG · BRUCE CABOT

A COOPER-SCHOEDSACK PRODUCTION—AN RKO RADIO PICTURE—of course!
From a Story by Edgar Wallace and Merian C. Cooper—David O. Selznick, Executive Producer
RKO RADIO PICTURES · RKO BUILDING · RADIO CITY · NEW YORK

WARD & GLYNNE'S
PATCHOGUE THEATRE
7 DAYS STARTING
SUNDAY AUG. 23
WITH VAUDEVILLE

CHARLIE CHAPLIN
IN "THE GOLD RUSH"

Cinema-going in **wartime** Norfolk

Carrie-Anne Elsden traces the effects of both world wars on Norfolk picture houses.

The Great War

When Britain declared war on Germany on 4 August 1914, there were around 3,500 cinemas nationwide. Though the austerity of the war period curtailed the building of luxury venues, swathes of smaller cinemas popped up all across the country, placing moving pictures within the reach of everyone.

New ventures in Norfolk capitalising on the growing popularity of film included the Regent and Central in Great Yarmouth, the Picture House in Diss, the Dereham & District Picture Palace, Sheringham's Picture House, the Electric Cinema in Burnham Market, The Regal in Cromer, The Cinema in Holt, Matthishall's Electric, the Electric Cinema in Watton, the Electric in Wells, the Picture House in Wymondham and the 'Thatched' in Norwich.

Although a large number of cinemas had opened, the war effort hindered their operations as many cinema employees were called to the front. Remaining staff had to fulfil multiple roles to keep cinemas open. Those called up included the pianists and musicians who provided the soundtrack to silent pictures. Ingeniously some of these were replaced by mechanised pianos or pianolos.

Among the first generation of cinema staff

INTERIOR OF THE THATCHED CINEMA BALLROOM 1904

BOMB DAMAGE NEAR THE REGAL CINEMA, NORWICH, 1942

The Second World War

Until war was declared on September 3, 1939, nothing had closed the cinemas. In fear of imminent bomb raids the government forced all picture houses to shut, but in the absence of enemy air attacks, audiences grew frustrated that they could not access their local cinema. The government soon realised that maintaining good morale was a crucial factor in helping to win the war. Cinemas offered the chance for much needed escapism, and also acted as an excellent channel for propaganda. As the war continued, cinema came to be valued so highly that projectionists over the age of 25, as well as film transport drivers, were excused from service.

After just one week of being out of action, cinemas across Norwich reopened - though they now operated under strict blackouts and external lights were forbidden until the end of the conflict. Some Norfolk cinemas were requisitioned, as they had been in the First World War, including the Gem in Great Yarmouth, and the Central on nearby Market Place served as a temporary Marks & Spencer when the town's branch was bombed in 1939. Meanwhile, the Electric Theatre in King's Lynn served as army barracks.

in the region whom were lost, was Archibald Page, commissionaire at the Empire in Norwich. He was wounded in battle and died in 1916, leaving behind his new wife and baby daughter. Some of Norfolk's picture houses were also requisitioned during the war; the building which later became the Thatched in Norwich initially served as a billet for troops in the early war years.

Drinking hours were restricted which encouraged more patrons to visit their local picture house, especially soldiers on leave. At the Theatre of Varieties in Cromer, patrons could enjoy films, live theatre and boxing; it became a popular retreat for soldiers billeted nearby. Charlie Chaplin, Harold Lloyd and Buster Keaton were beginning to come to the fore as firm audience favourites. The Clutching Hand was the box office favourite at the Empire in Norwich, a serial following the crafty exploits of the eponymous criminal.

In 1916, filmmakers captured bitter scenes of fighting at the Somme, specifically the battle where tanks were used for the very first time in warfare. The king announced: "The public should see these pictures that they may have some idea of what the army is doing, and what war means."

The feature-length documentary was unlike any of the newsreels the public had seen before and audiences flocked to their local picture house to see it. At the Picture House on Norwich's Haymarket, some 14,000 cinemagoers watched *Battle Of The Somme* in the film's opening week - the cinema had five showings a day during the week and six on a Saturday.

"At the Picture House on Norwich's Haymarket, some 14,000 cinemagoers watched Battle Of The Somme in the film's opening week."

THE BATTLE OF THE SOMME [BR 1916]

Credit Ronald Grant

East Anglia was transformed into a main base for aircraft activity, and became home not only to native servicemen but for those from around the world too. The Rex in Feltwell opened in 1940, hoping to attract patrons from the town's RAF station. Some airfields and army bases set up their own cinema screens, including RAF Feltwell, although this did not stop Eric Mills of Sheringham's Picture House from capitalising on the situation by offering mobile shows to other RAF and army camps around the region.

Many personnel still enjoyed visiting the local pictures houses and the Regent Cinema in Norwich boasted some very famous clientele, including Captain Clark Gable, of the 351st Bomb Group, and Major James Stewart, of the 445th Operations Group, who were both stationed at local airbases.

The presence of large numbers of military personnel resulted in the declaration of Emergency Regulation 42B: with the approval of the local authority, cinemas were allowed to open on Sundays for the first time. The Regal in Holt was the first cinema in Norfolk to action the emergency measure in 1940, which could explain why Baron Pert, the long-serving manager, considered the war years to be his best business ever. Many cinemagoers wanted Sunday screenings to continue when peacetime resumed; the decision often came down to a tense vote held by each local authority.

The war years were a boom period for cinema-going. Even as air-raid sirens blared during the Blitz, audience members were reluctant to leave their seats; the Odeon in Norwich had a siren on its roof but often patrons would not be moved.

City cinemas did not emerge unscathed however: in 1942 an unexploded bomb buried itself in the Carlton's outer wall; the Regal on Dereham Road had its roof blown off; and a bomb penetrated the Odeon despite the cinema having been made 'practically invisible' by a camouflage expert, who had painted two of the building's walls to look like rows of houses and disguised the entire rear car park with patches of red material to look like rooftops. Sadly some buildings were destroyed including the Thatched and the Empire on Oak Street, which were bombed during the Blitz in 1942.

Credit Picture Norfolk

AIR RAID DAMAGE TO THE ODEON CINEMA, NORWICH

JAMES STEWART

Credit Picture Norfolk

> The Regent Cinema in Norwich boasted some very famous clientele, including Captain Clark Gable, of the 351st Bomb Group, and Major James Stewart, of the 453rd Operations Group, who were both stationed at local airbases.

The boy projectionist

Mike Hutchinson remembers the teenage cinema entrepreneur who became a Norfolk sheriff.

An early entrepreneur in the Norwich cinema scene was young Alfred Warminger. In 1933, at the age of 13, he became manager of his own cinema specifically for children, The Globe, in a wooden hut behind his father's pub in the Elm Hill area of Norwich. Children sat on wooden seats after paying the 1d entrance money. Some box office assistance was provided by Alfred's sister Emily and friend Leonard Britcher, who was the commissionaire. In only a few months Alfred had made a profit of £70 and decided to branch out into a bigger cinema.

With his father's backing, he opened The Enterprise in Northumberland Street in 1934 with more seats. This cinema cost £1,500 and was equipped for sound films. A gala opening by the Norwich Lord Mayor Fred Jex drew the crowds and filled the 250 seat cinema; hundreds more were turned away. In later life Alfred recalled that the children especially enjoyed Charlie Chaplin and Laurel and Hardy.

Margery Dix remembers that the children were well-behaved and the atmosphere was a lot calmer than in the bigger city cinemas of the time. She also remembers seeing comedy films, westerns and a documentary about whales. In an EDP article, Maurice Middleton recalled that the entrance fee was a 1lb jam jar and a halfpenny, or a 2lb jar and a rabbit skin.

Eventually the premises were sold and became a slipper factory, which was demolished in 1987. Among the debris on the site was the original Enterprise sign.

As an adult, Alfred went on to bigger things. He took a mobile cinema around the county playing in village halls. In the Second World War, he served as a flight lieutenant.

THE GLOBE CINEMA
(A. WORMINGER, JUNR.)

GLOBE STREET, NORWICH
Telephone 726

The Norwich Boy Cinema Proprietor.

PROGRAMMES CHANGED WEEKLY

Every Evening at 6.30   Matinees Saturdays at 2 & 4 p.m.

Admission 1d.   A First Class Programme Always

The Morris Printing Co., Ltd., 36, Botolph Street, Norwich.

After leaving the RAF he continued flying as a glider pilot. In 1957, he achieved a record-breaking flight of almost 30,000ft, which is a height used by passenger jets today.

Alfred's mother, Mottie Warminger, became the landlady of the Ferry Boat pub in King Street in 1945 and presided over the bar "with queenly grace" for 30 years, until she was 85.

"Warminger Wants Waste Paper" was a slogan that everybody knew and Alfred became one of the biggest merchants in the country. In 1960, he became the Sheriff of Norwich and, after a very eventful life, he died in 1995.

Acknowledgements: Eastern Daily Press, Canberra Times, Lakes Gliding Club, Mrs M Dix, Frances and Michael Holmes (Norwich Pubs and Breweries Past and Present), David Cleveland.

The entrance fee was a 1lb jam jar and a halfpenny, or a 2lb jar and a rabbit skin.

High times

Ronald Green remembers his two-wheeled adventures in the name of cinema.

PROMOTION FOR THE FILM SMILEY (1956) FEATURING LEFT TO RIGHT, FREDDY KERRISON, PERCY (DODGER) KERRISON & ELSIE KERRISON

66 One of our cycles was called The Bedstead Bike and was made from the top of an old bed, brass knobs and all, by my uncles Percy "Dodger" Kerrison and Jimmy Clarke. I was the first to ride it – and the first to have an accident on it! 99

In the early 1950s I was part of the Dodgers Penny Farthing Cycling Club as well as the Old Time Cycles Club in Norwich and I was often called upon to ride cycles around the city to advertise what was showing at the cinema.

The Gaumont at that time was called The Carlton and we promoted films for them and for The Regent on Prince of Wales Road. We were also promoting Dodgers Cycles shop, which was on Chapel Street off Rupert Street. We'd just get two free cinema tickets

RON GREEN C.1953 ON
THE BEDSTEAD BIKE

PROMOTION FOR
THE FILM ISN'T LIFE
WONDERFUL (1953)
CYCLISTS INCLUDE
JUNE AND JOYCE HENRY
(RON'S SISTERS) AND
DOREEN CLARKE

PROMOTION INSIDE
THE REGENT CINEMA —
PRINCE OF WALES ROAD

as payment. One of our cycles was called The Bedstead Bike and was made from the top of an old bed, brass knobs and all, by my uncles Percy "Dodger" Kerrison and Jimmy Clarke. I was the first to ride it - and the first to have an accident on it!

I've seen a few photographs taken of us all inside and outside The Regent and The Carlton. One photo I remember is from outside The Regent. We'd all cycled from Rupert Street, and I'm on a penny farthing with a fake beard, with the cinema manager standing beside me. Dodger is on the back of a three-wheeled tandem and his brother Freddy is in pyjamas behind the Bedstead Bike, which I had three crashes on.

One film we advertised at The Regent was called *Smiley*, about a young Australian boy saving up to buy a bike. He nearly has enough then he keeps getting blamed for smashing a window and things like that and has to pay for them.

I can also recall my first visit to the cinema, The Empire in Oak Street. Shirley Temple was in one film and George Formby in the other - he lost his pet goldfish down

the gutter. This must have been 1939 as I remember seeing people diving off the Iron Bridge into the Wensum by the Old City Railway Station. George sang a song, Swim Little Fish Swim On.

As for the penny farthing, I once finished up in the Norfolk and Norwich Hospital. I was lucky that day. The police came round to my Gran's and asked who had the accident and what vehicle I was on. I told him it was a penny farthing and he didn't believe me. "Don't be cheeky!" he said. Everybody laughed except him.

Promotion for
the film Genevieve
(1953) at the Odeon,
Botolph Street

Promotion for The
Carlton/Gaumont
on All Saints Green

The **end** of an **era**

Basil Abbott, Manager of Diss Museum, shares his cinema memories.

I have a recurring dream that the Diss Picture House is open again. Even in my sleep I know this is not possible, because it closed for good on March 3, 1973. I was there that night to see a film about Darwin called *The Voyage Of The Beagle* and a Robert Redford and George Segal film, *How To Steal A Diamond In Four Uneasy Lessons* (known in the USA and on TV as *The Hot Rock*). When Redford sauntered off with the diamond at the end it was the close of an era for me.

In 1965, I went to the Picture House 50 times. Life was simpler in those days. Anyone who went to see films knew that the height of ambition, the goal of life, was to get the girl and a recording contract. My younger brother and I must have seen *Zulu* 10 times over the years and could probably supply the dialogue if the sound was turned down.

I realise now that it was not an accurate representation of Victorian times – but it was the best British action film of them all. We saw the first dozen or so Elvis Presley films, missing only *Wild In The Country*, until he started making rubbish. Time gave us the gift of judgment; did we really walk all that way, spend all that money and waste an evening watching Raquel Welch in *Fathom*?

In the 1950s, we would go on a Saturday morning. Old cinemas have a distinctive smell that still excites me. Jack Jones, the proprietor, would be there in his cap and our tickets would be taken by a girl who sometimes wore a cowboy hat. We cheered the heroes, booed the bad 'uns and heard the sound of rolling Coke bottles and cries of "Put a shillin' in the meter!" when the projector broke down. I can remember our bewilderment when Hopalong Cassidy

> "In 1965, I went to the Picture House 50 times. Life was simpler in those days. Anyone who went to see films knew that the height of ambition, the goal of life, was to get the girl and a recording contract."

Credit Ronald Grant

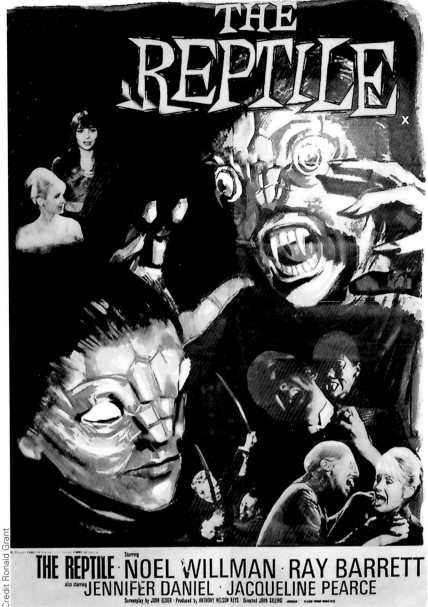

Credit Ronald Grant

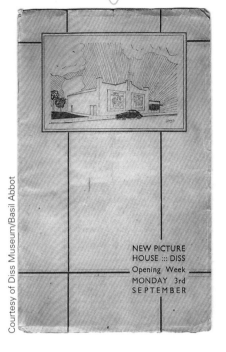

DISS PICTURE HOUSE
FRONT OF PROGRAMME
1934

NEW PICTURE
HOUSE ::: DISS
Opening Week
MONDAY 3rd
SEPTEMBER

Courtesy of Diss Museum/Basil Abbot

kissed a girl. "Why did Hoppy do that?" we wondered aloud as we walked home. I was often grumpy on the way home and was usually told by my parents: "You're tired." When you're young they always tell you that, even when you are not at all tired. I suppose I just resented being back in the rainy streets of Diss minutes after being in Sherwood Forest or defending *The Alamo*.

There were grumbles from the patrons on the way out if the film had been anything but straightforward tripe. *If...* and *Oh! What A Lovely War* caused moans of bewilderment.

The town's first cinema was built in 1916 and rebuilt in 1934, and the first film in the new building was *Evergreen* (1934), a talkie with Jessie Matthews. I remember the queues to see Cliff Richard in *The Young Ones*.

A dozen years later the place closed because nobody was going. Such is the fickleness of fashion. In the postwar years, there had been two houses every night as

cinema enjoyed a boom period.

Films are not the same on television. There is something special about a large, hushed audience watching a film in a cinema. Certainly horror films lose much of their impact. I had a sleepless night, at the age of 17, after seeing *The Reptile*. When I saw it again on television I wondered what had bothered me.

Poignant moments from films stick in my mind: the Borstal boys singing Jerusalem in *The Loneliness Of The Long Distance Runner*; the moment at the end of *The Great Escape* when the guard turns, touched by the sound of Steve McQueen's baseball tap-tapping against the "cooler" wall; the "freeze" on *Butch Cassidy And The Sundance Kid* as they fall to three volleys by half the Bolivian army.

I wish the Picture House was open again. As we came out, my brother Simon would say: "Good, wa'n't it?" When we got home, my mother would say: "Was it good? Many there?"

> ❝Films are not the same on television. There is something special about a large, hushed audience watching a film in a cinema.❞

Ghosts of cinemas past

Photographer **Nick Stone,** creator of the celebrated Blitz Ghosts and Great War Ghosts projects, was commissioned by Norfolk At The Pictures to explore the history of cinemas in Norwich and Great Yarmouth. These are the extraordinary results, with notes and explanations from Nick.

THE EMPIRE
GREAT YARMOUTH

ROYAL AQUARIUM,
GREAT YARMOUTH

THE GAUMONT,
NORWICH

Rephotography is a technique that has been in existence for a long time as a comparative method of relating the history of a landscape over time; ghosting images is a relatively new process, dating from around 2003 as a technique, and has flourished in the new form as software has developed to accommodate the technique.

It is about more than software though. If produced carefully and correctly ghosting can produce a real window into the past, giving the viewer a glimpse of how familiar scenes would have looked decades ago. It's also a learning experience for me, as a visual artist who is more than casually interested in heritage. You have to examine the area you are working in quite thoroughly to try and put yourself in the footprint of the original photographer. Often concentrating on finding elements in the photographs that line up with the modern scene to achieve the desired effect, simple things like angles and the distance between objects in the

REGENT
GREAT YARMOUTH

THE GEM
GREAT YARMOUTH

ODEON, NORWICH

MARINA PICTURE PALACE
GREAT YARMOUTH

THE REGAL
GREAT YARMOUTH

THEATRE ROYAL
GREAT YARMOUTH

background can be key in trying to position yourself correctly, as well as a working knowledge of focal lengths and how modern lenses distort what you see. It all has to be corrected to achieve the effect of standing further back from a scene to get peripheral information in.

I also enjoy examining the original photos, quite often you end up with a real sense of how things have changed beyond the obvious and start to understand the urban landscape better - how the streets worked, what other building and businesses operated in the area, how the area has changed and the effects on the local community. This is particularly true of cinemas, which often were at the heart of a community along with pubs.

The first series for Norfolk at the Pictures were very successful, just featuring cinemas in Norwich. Despite having what I thought was a reasonable understanding of the history of cinema in the city, it has been an education for me, the heritage of cinema in the city is strong and varied and encompasses areas where now you'd

The Picture House/
Haymarket/
Gaumont, Norwich

The Picture House/
Haymarket/
Gaumont, Norwich

THE PICTURE HOUSE/ HAYMARKET/ GAUMONT, NORWICH

ABC NORWICH

not necessarily realise there was ever a cinema such as The Mayfair in Magdalen Street which stood where Epic is now, or the Haymarket/Gaumont where Topshop currently stands, neither of which exist at all as both were demolished to make way for new developments.

These images are threaded together from the street line or the position of buildings around them, backed up by research using maps and details of addresses plus the street archaeology of building lines and boundaries. Others like the ABC on Prince of Wales Road present a familiar facade but detailing has changed over time.

Working in the second series in Great Yarmouth was nice. I know the town quite well but learnt a lot more just by walking between the nine sites of the cinemas. The surviving buildings are rather beautiful, in particular The Empire, which despite bits of the facade being damaged and being removed still stands out on Marine Parade as an iconic piece of architecture. Cinemas like the Regent still exist as buildings whereas the Regal up in the town was demolished and presented some problems with location.

The Hollywood, formerly the Royalty, and The Royal Aquarium provided a nice opportunity to create ghosts from several time periods - it has a long history as an entertainment centre and a cinema, one of the few buildings in the town that has fairly consistently been in use for entertainment for most of the last century.

Norwich's **premier** cinema

Marc Atkinson charts the life of Norwich's
ABC cinema and the career of one of its most
famous managers, **Bryan Waters.**

BRYAN WALTERS
OUTSIDE THE
ABC CINEMA

Bryan Waters was part of the cinema business all his working life and a fixture on the Norwich entertainment scene for more than 20 years.

His career began with the prestigious Odeon chain, where he commenced training at the Odeon in Dagenham, Stroud and Gants Hill. Later in his career he became a mobile manager for the rival ABC (Associated British Cinemas) chain and was at the forefront of innovations in cinema exhibition for over 30 years.

In the early 1970s, some of the ABC cinemas in London began to close in response to the impact of television and declining audiences. A hugely popular cinema chain with many venues since the late 1920s, the closures left many displaced cinema managers. Having spent his career as a mobile manager in or around cinemas in London, Bryan made the decision of settling his family down in a more firmly established cinema venue.

As luck would have it, a position became available at the ABC in Norwich on Prince Of Wales Road, and after a successful application, Bryan and his wife moved to Norfolk where they have lived ever since.

The Norwich ABC began life as The Regent in 1923. Perhaps the city's most spectacular cinema it went on to also become the city's longest running. It was developed by celebrated local cinema magnate Frederick Holmes Cooper. It originally had 1,800 seats and was equipped for variety acts as well as moving pictures. It was a very ambitious and ornate building, with elaborate decor including a fountain (complete with goldfish) in the foyer. It even had a resident orchestra, waiting area for patrons and a parking service. The Regent was taken over by ABC as early as 1929.

By 1961, however, the cinema had been extensively modernised and in 1971 was converted from one to three screens to become East Anglia's first multi-screen venue. The ABC was still, however, a large and spectacular building, and it included a range of flats for managers and staff in the upper floors, formerly Alexandra Mansions.

Bryan expected working in Norwich to be easier than his experiences in London where he would often have to employ an off-duty police officer to sit in on screenings, but Norwich had its own challenges. One of his first problems were the boisterous groups of teenagers that frequented the cinema. On Bryan's third day in the job, one

> **"**The Norwich ABC began life as The Regent in 1923. Perhaps the city's most spectacular cinema it went on to also become the city's longest-running.**"**

particular group tried to sneak in without buying enough tickets. Recognising this as a common occurrence, Bryan decided to lay down the law literally and called the police and eventually took them to court. Bryan had made his mark immediately and as word got round that a new manager was in town there was less trouble at the cinema and his exploits even got him into the local paper creating publicity for the cinema.

Bryan became a well-known local personality and worked hard with his staff to promote and innovate at the cinema. He developed the bar within the venue and established late shows and all-nighters in the late 70s, featuring horror and kung-fu films. If customers could make it through the night they could treat themselves to a cooked breakfast at the cinema's refurbished café, known as the Grillette.

The screenings he established for schools also became so popular that Bryan would have to inform the police to guide the traffic for certain shows as the Prince of Wales Road became blocked up by school buses.

THE GRILETTE AT
THE NORWICH ABC
CINEMA IN THE 1960s

The ABC chain was well known for their Saturday morning kids' club - the ABC Minors - and Norwich children were entertained at the ABC by Little and Large, The Krankies and Olly Day among others.

It was during this time that a young Trevor Wicks worked at the cinema - Trevor later developed the Hollywood chain of cinemas including the former Odeon venue at Anglia Square.

Bryan came up with many other ideas to make the cinema a success. Noting the popularity of the venue with young people he added pool tables and a jukebox in the bar. Later he was one of the first managers to see the potential in modern forms of amusement and he added fruit machines and arcade games to the cinema foyer and other spaces.

There were troubled times as well: on one occasion Bryan was called out in the middle of the night after a fire had been started by someone lighting newspaper stuffed into the cinema seats. Screens Two and Three were affected and the doors broken where the arsonist had tried to escape. The residents of the surrounding buildings came out in their night clothes to see the cinema ablaze. Despite the damage, Bryan was able to keep Screen One open while the rest of the building was repaired.

The cinema continued successfully into

DRACULA
PRINCE OF DARKNESS

CHRISTOPHER LEE · BARBARA SHELLEY · ANDREW KEIR

FRANCIS MATTHEWS · SUZAN FARMER · CHARLES TINGWELL
THORLEY WALTERS

Credit Ronald Grant Archive

66 He developed the bar within the venue and established late shows and all-nighters in the late 70s, featuring horror and kung-fu films. 99

ABC MINORS
ANNIVERSARY
PARTY 1962

ABC
BAR

THE QUEEN
MOTHER AT
ABC CINEMA
NORWICH
1971

the 1970s, with a Royal premiere of *The Go Between* attended by the Queen Mother in 1971, and a fourth screen was introduced where the restaurant had originally stood. Screen Four featured 74 luxury seats and even trialed a new system called "video" for a brief time. Incredibly, video was considered a viable format for the future of cinema projection at the time. Bryan had no end of problems with the new technology, however, which was constantly breaking down and provided a very low picture and sound quality. Video technology, of course, never took off and standard projection equipment was later installed.

The ABC was later taken over by the Cannon Cinemas chain in 1986, and finally the Virgin group before closing in the late 90s. Bryan decided to retire early from cinema management after running it successfully for 22 years and receiving many awards for his innovations and hard work. The building is still used for entertainment, however, housing the Mercy nightclub with the Grillete now an independent fast-food retailer. If you turn the corner, you can still see evidence of its former use with a stone carved sign of The Regent Theatre hanging above a row of houses and names carved into the brick where for decades people would queue along the streets to get into one of Norwich's favourite cinemas.

Cinema memories
Norwich

Lucy Cowburn talks to **Peter Cossey** about rock'n'roll teens and the onset of 3D.

In 1946, 1.6 billion people visited the cinema; these figures steadily dropped over the next two decades and by 1969 had fallen to 214 million. In Norwich, the number of cinemas decreased from 11 in 1950 to just four by 1960. In its cinema heyday, Norwich had four circuit cinemas, a handful of local ones and a couple of independents - many of which had closed by the beginning of the 1960s. While the reason for this sharp change is generally credited to television, the absence of adults in cinema seats meant that a whole new market could open up: teenagers. Here Peter Cossey, owner of The Movie Shop in Norwich, shares his memories of the time...

Even before the time of teens, cinemas had their young audiences in mind. There would be Saturday morning performances, referred to as sixpenny rushes, directly aimed at children. These were primarily made up of serials and comedy shorts followed by a big picture, usually a western. Two trips to the cinema in one day was not uncommon at this time. The chance to win free drinks and the promise of sticky toffees at Christmas kept the customers coming back.

The teenage phenomenon hit Norwich in 1957. It was a cultural shift that had started in America a couple of years previously with James Dean, Marlon Brando and Elvis Presley leading the way. Elvis, particularly, made an impression on Norwich audiences. When *Loving You* was released, with Elvis in full colour and accompanied by all his hits, the cinema was absolutely packed. After the show, the crowd of young people continued to mill around the Haymarket cinema due to an electric atmosphere and a sense that something was about to change. This was followed in the same year by *Rock Around the Clock*. On its closing night at The Regal Cinema, the crowd ran wild. There was dancing in the aisles and once they left the cinema the police were called to calm the overexcited teenagers.

The link between cinema and rock'n'roll

> **66** The teenage phenomenon hit Norwich in 1957. It was a cultural shift that had started in America a couple of years previously with James Dean, Marlon Brando and Elvis Presley leading the way. **99**

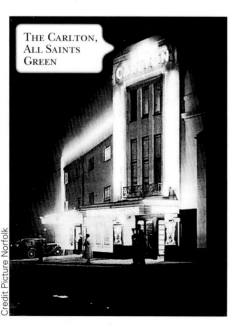

THE CARLTON, ALL SAINTS GREEN

Credit Picture Norfolk

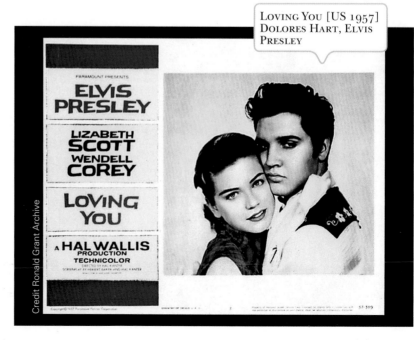

LOVING YOU [US 1957] DOLORES HART, ELVIS PRESLEY

Credit Ronald Grant Archive

GAUMONT, ALL
SAINTS GREEN
SAT CLUB 1972

66 The peak of the trend, in Norwich at least, was in 1964 when The Rolling Stones played to screaming fans at the Gaumont Cinema. 99

continued in both the UK and America – Beatles films such as *A Hard Day's Night* got Hollywood backing as the teenage market grew. The peak of the trend, in Norwich at least, was in 1964 when The Rolling Stones played to screaming fans at the Gaumont Cinema.

There being little else to do in an evening, the local cinemas quickly became hangouts for teenagers. Cinema owners soon realised that teenagers were their biggest audience, and they adapted accordingly. Cheap exploitation and sexploitation films were shown more frequently; The Aquarium in Great Yarmouth would even show unrated or banned films. Although there was nothing of this rank in Norwich, the Norvic Cinema was a popular spot for Friday nights, showing pure schlock. Its line-up frequently included sci-fi and juvenile delinquent Z-movies.

Cinema-going for teens at that time was about more than just the films, though. In fact, these were often all but ignored in favour of socialising and meeting the opposite sex. Teenagers only ventured to the more respectable circuit cinemas when trying to impress a date.

It wasn't just the allure of rock'n'roll or the chance to socialise that enticed people; gimmicks were also employed. In Norwich this started around 1953 at the Regal. The cinema started showing 3D films and, although these were predominantly B-movies, the manager decided on at least one occasion to give a 40-odd minute documentary top billing over a Kirk Douglas piece. It also implemented widescreen, of a sort, to attract people. Unable to afford the necessary projection equipment for widescreen and CinemaScope, he simply altered the aspect ratio of standard film using a special lens. This was advertised as a panoramic screen but, in reality, lead to the top and the bottom of the image being cut off and a good deal of headless actors.

Peter Cossey's book, Norwich Cinemas 1946-1960, is out now.

PRINCE OF WALES
ROAD, NORVIC
FORMERLY ELECTRIC
JUNE 10 1961

A HARD DAYS NIGHT
[BR 1964] WITH THE
BEATLES AND WILFRED
BRAMBELL

My life as a
projectionist

David Cleveland, formerly a member of the on-screen team on the BBC Television show Vision On and founder of the East Anglian Film Archive, recalls how his life-long passion for film and the cinema was formed working at the Norvic in Norwich and Regal in North Walsham in the 50s and 60s.

I started as third projectionist at the Norvic cinema in Prince of Wales Road in the spring of 1959. As it was my first full time job I can remember distinctly the day-to-day running. The main staff consisted of Mr Mathews the manager, a cashier, a confectionery sales person, a commissionaire and three projectionists. In addition there were usherettes who doubled as Wall's ice cream, Butterkist and Kia-Ora sales girls during the intervals.

The first to arrive in the morning, just after 9am, were the projectionists who had a number of duties such as maintaining the projectors, making up the rolls of film ready for the next change of programme, putting up posters on the front canopy, maintaining electrical equipment and lights in the cinema and cleaning brass fittings. Mr Mathews would also arrive, and at about eleven there was a tea break in the cafe opposite in Eastbourne Place.

Lunch was from about 12.30 to 1.30, when the operators (as projectionists were called) returned - first having to light the small gas lamps around the auditorium which were the secondary lighting (alight all the time by law in case the electricity failed), then lacing the projectors and preparing the arc light ready for the show. Normally this commenced about 1.45, depending on the running time of

NORWICH, NORVIC CINEMA

the films for the day's programme. The doors opened and the patrons came in - sitting either downstairs (1/9 at the front, 2/9 at the rear) or upstairs in the circle where the prices were 3/6 at the front and 2/9 at the back.

The continuous programme would consist of a second feature, shorts and adverts, trailers and sales, then the main feature. These had already been assembled by the operators in the right order, with appropriate titles such as "Next Week" and "Sunday Only" for the trailers. The reels of film, each running about 20 minutes, were numbered and stored in order ready to be laced up and changed over as the programme progressed.

The presentation - the lowering and raising of the house lights and footlights, the opening and closing of the curtains, the correct black masking for the picture ratio, the fading down and up of recorded music from the non-synchronous 78rpm turntables, as well as focusing, framing (or racking) of the picture, correct adjustment of the arc light so that it did not change colour or go dim - all this was part of the projectionist's job. The order of the short interest films, advertisements, trailers and so on was also the projectionist's responsibly, and these were carefully arranged to give a smooth performance both in picture and sound. Some cinemas had newsreels as well which lasted for three days before being replaced with a more up-to-date edition. Occasionally the newsreels had an additional, often local story which was rushed to the cinema to be added to the existing print.

Apart from four or five minute intervals between features, the programme ran continuously through to about 10pm or sometimes later, when the last item to be shown was *The Queen*, a short film of a picture of the monarch and the God Save the Queen music for about 30 seconds. Then the audience filed out, the auditorium was checked for lighted cigarette ends or anything else left behind. Then it was out

with the lights and locking up. If it was a Saturday night the films had to be spooled off onto cores and packed into cans ready for the Film Transport van to collect to take them to another cinema for the next week.

The Norvic closed in 1961, as did many other cinemas around this time due to the introduction of television to East Anglia - both Anglia Television and BBC East began in October 1959.

During those last few weeks of the Norvic fellow projectionist Geoff Clarke and I both made films of the cinema, which are now in the East Anglian Film Archive. I was moved by Victor Harrison, the owner of the Norvic, to another of his cinemas, the Regal at North Walsham, and Geoff went to Harrison's Stowmarket cinema.

At North Walsham the running of the cinema was different, with only one daily programme, beginning at 7pm. Normally there was a "Sunday Only" film, then a different programme for Monday, Tuesday and Wednesday, and another for Thursday Friday and Saturday. Occasionally, a big film would be given a week's run.

The audience was mainly made up of regulars who came once or twice a week regardless of what was showing. Some couples even sat in the same seats. Then there were those who wanted to see a particular film, and would ring up for details, or book seats at the "Workbox", a small haberdashery shop in the centre of town.

From 1961 to the spring of 1963, I was the only projectionist seeing to all the making up and breaking down of the films, maintenance work, and showing the films. A youngster was trained up to cover days off. Afternoons were normally free, and this enabled me to pursue my interests of exploring the local countryside by bike, pursuing local history and making 16mm films - which led to a BBC training scheme and a life of film-making and film archive work. The Regal North Walsham continued until 1978.

> **"**
> The Norvic closed in 1961, as did many other cinemas around this time due to the introduction of television to East Anglia – both Anglia Television and BBC East began in October 1959.**"**

Norwich and Great Yarmouth
at the Pictures

Mike Hutchinson looks back at a varied history of Norfolk cinema-going in the city and on the coast.

Credit Percy Trett Collection

CENTRAL CINEMA OPENED 1915, RENAMED THE PLAZA IN 1928. PERCY TRETT COLLECTION

ELECTRIC CINEMA PRINCE OF WALES ROAD 1920

Credit Picture Norfolk

The people of Norfolk had their first taste of the miracle of moving pictures back in the 1890s, when Victoria was still queen. When the first commercially produced projectors appeared entrepreneurs were ready and waiting to show what they could do to the public, and make some money in the process. The projectors were hand-cranked and crude by today's standards. Pictures flickered and of course there was no colour or sound, but the public flocked to see this miracle of modern science. Performances would not be in the luxurious surroundings of a cosy cinema.

Early films were first shown as sideshow attractions at the Tombland Fair or as part of Gilbert's Modern Circus of Varieties in the Agricultural Hall, in between the live acts. On Boxing Day 1897, ironically in the building which is now home to ITV Anglia, Norwich citizens witnessed a diverse collection of early documentary shorts, including the Derby, boxing kangaroos, railway trains, a match with Norfolk prizefighter Jem Mace and a royal garden party.

Pictures were short, but that didn't matter - they moved. That was the magic. Local scenes were always popular; everyone wanted to see themselves up on the big screen, even if it was just a few seconds as they walked out of a local factory or sat on Great Yarmouth seafront.

The Royal Aquarium.
Percy Trett
Collection

Kids club at
The Empire
Great Yarmouth

STAFF OUTSIDE
THE EMPIRE
CINEMA

DEREHAM ROAD
REGAL CINEMA
DAY AFTER OPENING
17 APRIL 1938

ST ANDREW ST
THEATRE DE LUXE
AT NIGHT,
30 NOVEMBER 1934

SANDWICHMEN
AT HAYMARKET
CINEMA

First cinemas

By the early 1900s, more permanent venues
were to be found, often in existing buildings
such as the Victoria Hall in St Stephen's
Street. Great Yarmouth was among the first
towns in the country to open a purpose-
built cinema, The Gem, described as "The
Palace of 5,000 Lights" (it actually had about
1,000). Still standing today, now called
The Windmill, the original cinema opened
in 1908. The manager, a young Charles
Cochran, later knighted for services to the
theatre business, invited people to come in
"when they liked and stay for as long as they
liked". Great Yarmouth council feared the
dreadful prospect of men and women sitting
in the dark all day, and insisted they sit at
opposite sides of the aisle.

Norwich opened its Theatre De Luxe
in 1910. By this time, film production had
become a more sophisticated industry,
with romance, adventure and mysteries,
accompanied by live piano. At the Thatched
cinema in All Saints Green, and at the
Gaumont in the Haymarket, small orchestras
were employed.

NORWICH, ST. GILES'
STREET, HIPPODROME
THEATRE, THE LAST
INTERIOR PHOTOGRAPH,
TAKEN BY GEORGE SWAIN
- 1960

The Gaumont in
the Haymarket,
Norwich

Credit Picture Norfolk

In Norwich and Great Yarmouth the race
was on to build bigger and more luxurious
cinemas. The capacity in many venues
exceeded 1,000 seats. Inside, the walls
were decorated with elaborate coloured
plasterwork in renaissance or Edwardian
styles. Exteriors were just as ornate, with no
expense spared. By the mid 1920s, Norwich
had 12 major cinemas and several smaller
establishments. Great Yarmouth had seven
cinemas - four remain standing today,
although only one is still a cinema.

Many of the buildings were designed to
accommodate live shows as well as films.
In Great Yarmouth summer visitors were
treated to performances from Gracie Fields
and George Formby, and a young Charlie
Chaplin is believed to have performed at the
Hippodromes in both Great Yarmouth and
Norwich. Laurel and Hardy also performed at
the Norwich Hippodrome, and many 1960s
pop stars, including The Beatles and The
Rolling Stones, played in Great Yarmouth
and Norwich.

> 66 The audience at the original Odeon in Botolph Street often stayed in their seats even as the air-raid siren on the roof sounded, warning them to go to shelters. 99

THE ODEON,
BOTOLPH STREET,
NORWICH

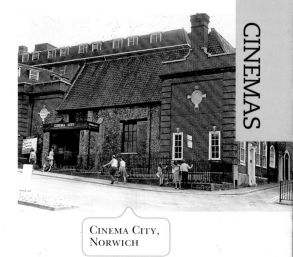

CINEMA CITY,
NORWICH

Heydays

The early 1930s were a turning point for the cinema industry, with the introduction of talking pictures. Some cinemas were slow to convert their premises, perhaps thinking it was a passing phase and an expensive one, and others closed their doors. New cinemas equipped with the new technology appeared, including The Carlton, The Regal and The Ritz in Norwich and The Regal in Great Yarmouth. Eventually, the pianists and cinema orchestras found themselves out of business, replaced by talkies and magnificent cinema organs which produced sound effects as well as music. Soon they in turn became redundant.

After the war, cinemas struggled to retain their audiences. Television was starting to be a real competitor and people often preferred to stay at home. The Odeon was replaced by a smaller cinema in 1971. Two other additions were The Noverre in Theatre Street and Cinema City, close to where the Theatre De Luxe once stood in St Andrew's Street.

One after another, cinemas closed their doors and were either torn down or, temporarily, turned into bingo halls. Those that remained were converted to multi-screens which often removed the splendour of the original decor and took the heart out of the building.

The old labour-intensive projectors have been replaced with digital machines. But in spite of modern developments in home entertainment, people are still "going to the pictures", and while Norwich and Great Yarmouth no longer have a multitude of cinemas they still have something like 30 screens between them in the ones that remain. What also remains is the enormous number of fond memories of how the cinema used to be when you settled down in the 1/9s, sipping from your carton of Kia-Ora as the smoke-enveloped projector beam hit the big screen.

Credit Picture Norfolk

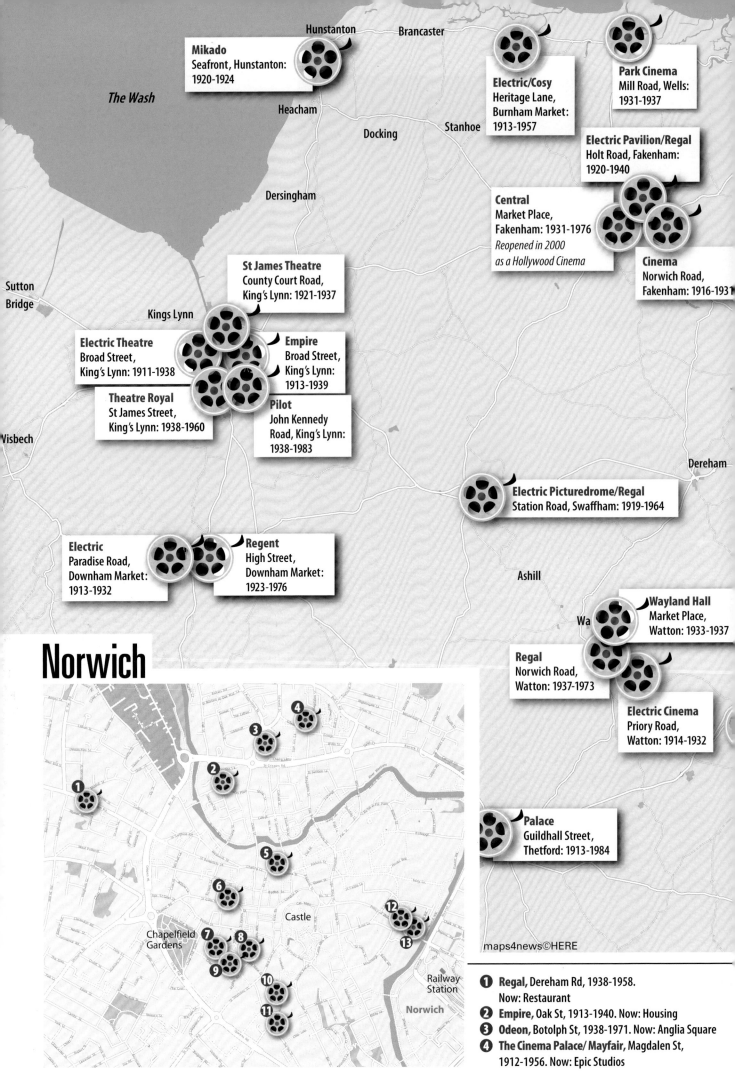

Mikado
Seafront, Hunstanton:
1920-1924

The Wash

Electric/Cosy
Heritage Lane,
Burnham Market:
1913-1957

Park Cinema
Mill Road, Wells:
1931-1937

Electric Pavilion/Regal
Holt Road, Fakenham:
1920-1940

Central
Market Place,
Fakenham: 1931-1976
*Reopened in 2000
as a Hollywood Cinema*

Cinema
Norwich Road,
Fakenham: 1916-1931

St James Theatre
County Court Road,
King's Lynn: 1921-1937

Electric Theatre
Broad Street,
King's Lynn: 1911-1938

Empire
Broad Street,
King's Lynn:
1913-1939

Theatre Royal
St James Street,
King's Lynn: 1938-1960

Pilot
John Kennedy
Road, King's Lynn:
1938-1983

Electric Picturedrome/Regal
Station Road, Swaffham: 1919-1964

Electric
Paradise Road,
Downham Market:
1913-1932

Regent
High Street,
Downham Market:
1923-1976

Wayland Hall
Market Place,
Watton: 1933-1937

Regal
Norwich Road,
Watton: 1937-1973

Electric Cinema
Priory Road,
Watton: 1914-1932

Palace
Guildhall Street,
Thetford: 1913-1984

Norwich

maps4news©HERE

❶ **Regal**, Dereham Rd, 1938-1958.
Now: Restaurant

❷ **Empire**, Oak St, 1913-1940. Now: Housing

❸ **Odeon**, Botolph St, 1938-1971. Now: Anglia Square

❹ **The Cinema Palace/ Mayfair**, Magdalen St,
1912-1956. Now: Epic Studios

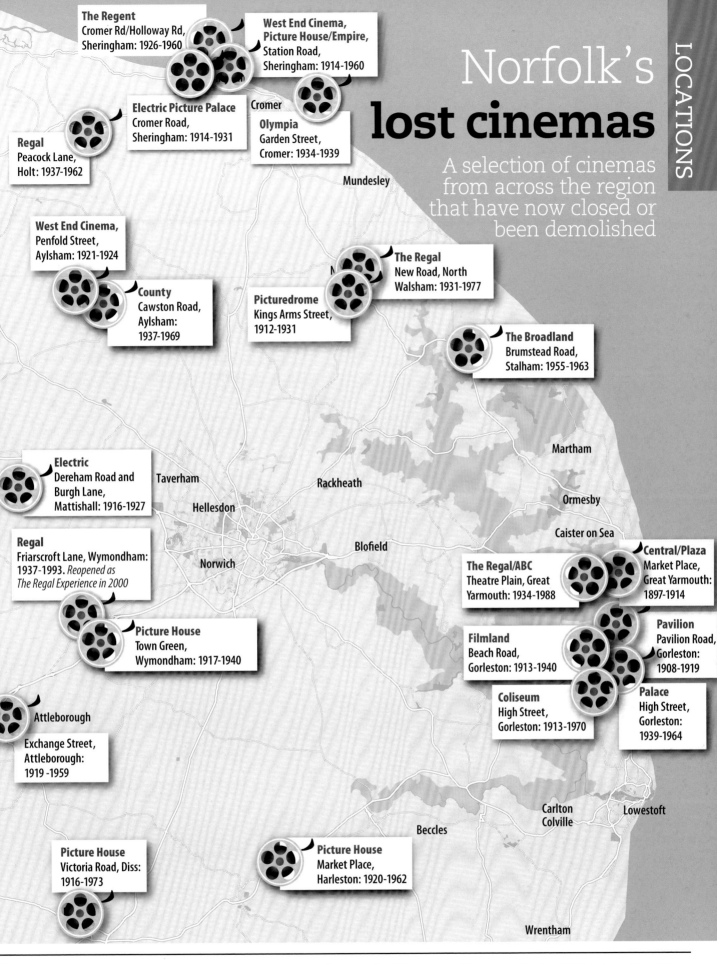

Norfolk's lost cinemas

A selection of cinemas from across the region that have now closed or been demolished

The Regent
Cromer Rd/Holloway Rd,
Sheringham: 1926-1960

**West End Cinema,
Picture House/Empire,**
Station Road,
Sheringham: 1914-1960

Electric Picture Palace
Cromer Road,
Sheringham: 1914-1931

Cromer

Olympia
Garden Street,
Cromer: 1934-1939

Regal
Peacock Lane,
Holt: 1937-1962

Mundesley

West End Cinema,
Penfold Street,
Aylsham: 1921-1924

County
Cawston Road,
Aylsham:
1937-1969

The Regal
New Road, North
Walsham: 1931-1977

Picturedrome
Kings Arms Street,
1912-1931

The Broadland
Brumstead Road,
Stalham: 1955-1963

Martham

Electric
Dereham Road and
Burgh Lane,
Mattishall: 1916-1927

Taverham

Rackheath

Ormesby

Hellesdon

Caister on Sea

Regal
Friarscroft Lane, Wymondham:
1937-1993. *Reopened as
The Regal Experience in 2000*

Norwich

Blofield

The Regal/ABC
Theatre Plain, Great
Yarmouth: 1934-1988

Central/Plaza
Market Place,
Great Yarmouth:
1897-1914

Picture House
Town Green,
Wymondham: 1917-1940

Filmland
Beach Road,
Gorleston: 1913-1940

Pavilion
Pavilion Road,
Gorleston:
1908-1919

Coliseum
High Street,
Gorleston: 1913-1970

Palace
High Street,
Gorleston:
1939-1964

Attleborough
Exchange Street,
Attleborough:
1919-1959

Carlton
Colville

Lowestoft

Beccles

Picture House
Victoria Road, Diss:
1916-1973

Picture House
Market Place,
Harleston: 1920-1962

Wrentham

---

⑤ **Theatre De Luxe**, St Andrews St,
1910-1970. Now: A car park

⑥ **The Hippodrome**, St Giles, 1903-1960
Now: A car park

⑦ **Theatre Royal**, Theatre St, 1956-1985
Now: Theatre Royal

⑧ **The Picture House/Gaumont**, Hay Hill,
1911-1959. Now: Site of Next Store

⑨ **Noverre**, Theatre St, 1950-1992
Now: Function room in the Assembly House

⑩ **The Carlton**, All Saints Green, 1932-1973
Now: Former Mecca Bingo Site

⑪ **Thatched Theatre**, All Saints Green, 1915-1930
Now: Near the site of John Lewis

⑫ **Electric (The Norvic)**, Prince of Wales Rd, 1912-1961
Now: A block of modern offices

⑬ **Prince of Wales**, Prince of Wales Rd, 1912-1922
Now: Grosvenor House

Market town glamour

Denis Bishop remembers The Regal in Watton.

> **The usherettes were local ladies who knew everyone, and I'm sure they reported back to our parents when they deemed it necessary!**

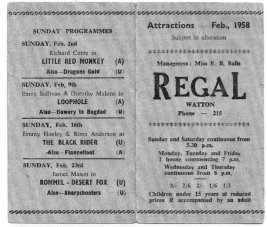

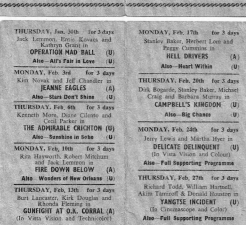

The Regal was built in 1937, and operated as a cinema until 1973. I remember the thrill of going to such an impressive cinema in a small market town like Watton.

The decoration was spectacular - plush seats, thick carpet, wonderful lighting - amazing for the 1950s and 60s. The building stood on Norwich Road, halfway between the police station and the railway station, with a long low old wartime building to the right which was used at one time as a clothing factory. Large trees surrounded the site and on the road frontage were white posts just wide enough for a car to access the car park. Also on the right hand boundary was the cycle shed.

A grand canopy hovered over six wide steps with the glass entrance at the top. We queued on the steps early to get the best seats. Over the canopy, the REGAL letters were illuminated at night. To the right of the canopy were the two display boards which announced the films for the current and next week. There was always an A and a B film each night with trailers for future films and a newsreel from Pathé. Down each side of the building were two exits. The foyer had the ticket office and ladies' toilet on the left with the main swing door into the auditorium in the centre and the manager's office and the gents' on the right. Also on the right was the access to the projection room over the foyer.

The usherettes were local ladies who knew everyone, and I'm sure they reported back to our parents when they deemed it necessary! The manager was strict and often took boys out for making noise. I remember it all: the soft pop-up seats, queuing with friends outside before it opened, being shown to your seat by an usherette, ice creams at the interval, coming out into the light after being in the dark for so long, the Pathé newsreels, trailers, the B movie first... and then the full feature. Of course, the girls were always in one row and the boys in the row behind.

The cinema was open every night except for Monday, and on Saturday mornings for children. Cowboys and Indians films were our favourites. The top names were Roy Rogers, Tom Mix and Hopalong Cassidy, then later John Wayne and Alan Ladd. My favourite film for many years was *Calamity Jane* - I loved Doris Day.

I was allowed to go to the cinema on Saturday mornings with my friends from the age of about seven. It was an adventure. Cycle to the cinema, meet friends on the way, park your cycle in the shed and then go into this dimly lit huge cinema and wait for the film. No trailers and no newsreel on a Saturday, just the main film. Cartoons like *Mickey Mouse* and *Popeye* and films with Charlie Chaplin and Laurel and Hardy.

Later we went in the evenings, usually on a Friday, and saw more grown-up films like *Red River, The Lavender Hill Mob* and, of course, *Calamity Jane*.

As teenagers, things were more serious and taking girls to the pictures was a very big step. First we would go as two groups, boys and girls. Then we would often pair up and some were left out at times - a difficult experience. We must have been to the cinema every week for years, and we saw hundreds of films there in the 1950s. I also remember that the local school used the cinema as a venue for its prize-giving day. It was the only venue in town that could seat the full school. When the cinema finally closed, it was empty for many years and then used as a camping holiday business and a removal and storage business. It was finally demolished and houses were built there instead.

Cinema memories
Holt

John Jarvis recalls a Saturday in 1950 when his love affair with the cinema began.

1936. REGAL HOLT UNDER CONSTUCTION

M y great-uncle Jack was the projectionist at The Electric Pavillion in Holt in the 1920s when films were silent and the projector was hand-cranked. He told me that if he wanted to get away quickly to see his girlfriend, he would turn the handle faster so the film would finish earlier.

The Regal in Holt was built by Douglas Bostock and opened in 1937. It was built to the same design as the Regal cinemas in Watton and Wymondham, which were part of the same circuit.

In 1937, a performer called Yodelling Reggie performed at the cinema. He used to play a mouth organ and yodel at the same time. He became quite famous and was even on the radio. His younger brother Archie became the projectionist at Holt cinema. Archie let me go up to the projection room on Saturday, May 25, 1950 when the manager had gone home for his tea. The film showing was *Christopher Columbus*, starring

Frederic March. I thought the experience was wonderful.

I was born and lived almost opposite the cinema and I could see the queues along the street from my window. I first went to the Regal with my mother and grandfather during the war when I was three to see *Snow White And The Seven Dwarfs*.

From 1948, I went three times a week without fail up until it closed. Regardless of what was on, I was there as was everyone, because it was the place to go. When television came into the house my parents and grandparents stopped going, but it didn't stop me. They would only go for a family trip when something big came out like *Carousel* or *The King And I*.

1937. REGAL HOLT MILLIE READ. FIRST USHERETTE.

HIS FIRST
FULL LENGTH
FEATURE
PRODUCTION !

Walt DISNEY'S

Snow White
and the Seven Dwarfs

in the Marvelous
MULTIPLANE
TECHNICOLOR

©W.D.P.

Christmas Eve in
the dwarfs'
cottage.

COUNTRY OF ORIGIN U.S.A.

HOLT CARNIVAL
STAFF OUTSIDE THE
REGAL IN 1957

SNOW WHITE AND
THE SEVEN DWARFS
[US 1937]

I really remember the later part of the 50s at The Regal, and they were wonderful times when there were a lot of people in there. I know there was smoking, but you could see the beam in the smoke. Sometimes if the film was a bit boring and it was Technicolor, the beam would be flashing different colours in the smoke and that would be just as interesting as the film.

From the early 60s, they tried the big epics like *El Cid* to draw people back in. My parents would watch these. There were also a lot of awful sword-and-sandals films from Italy, and spaghetti westerns. The only good ones were the ones with Clint Eastwood.

I can remember so many things about The Regal. I saw Elvis in *Love Me Tender*, where Elvis dies at the end and his ghost is standing beside a tree. All of the girls walked back home up the lane crying their eyes out. I remember seeing *Grand Prix* and afterwards everyone was driving up the road revving their engines. We saw *West Side Story* and came out of the film and it had snowed and four of us walked up the road arm-in-arm singing the songs.

The film that had the most showings at Holt was *Rock Around The Clock*. It had three

66 The Regal in Holt was built by Douglas Bostock and opened in 1937. It was built to the same design as the Regal cinemas in Watton and Wymondham, which were part of the same circuit. 99

more showings than any other film a week. It already had a reputation, as there were reports of people slashing cinema seats and riots in the street. Our local bobby sat at the back with his helmet in his lap. What he would have done if 500 of us had started anything... well, most likely he would have run for his life. His presence was definitely a deterrent, though.

My main cinema was Holt, but I was such a cinema fanatic that sometimes as well as going to the Holt Regal three times a week, I would go with a gang of friends to The Regent or the Picturehouse in Sheringham. I used to go to Cromer and Wells and couldn't believe that although the front was different the interior of Wells was exactly the same as Holt and Wymondham, because it was part of the same circuit. The only time I changed my cinema-going habits was when *Rawhide* starting showing on TV on Thursday nights.

I also became one of the projectionists at The Regal from 1964 until 1967, just before the cinema closed - nothing to do with me! I remember having to change the reels every 20 minutes. My most frightening experience was when we were showing *The Flight Of The Phoenix*; I had one reel running and I went to lace the second reel up and it fell out of my hands. It rolled around the projection room a couple of times, down the stairs and into the yard. I frantically got the reel back together just in time for the switchover.

When the Holt cinema closed down I would meet some friends in a cafe on a Sunday and decide what to see. If we went to Norwich we would make a day of it and go to a Wimpy bar, have our tea, and then go on to the Gaumont. I feel sad about the loss of

Credit Ronald Grant Archive

that cinema in particular as I saw a lot of big films there, including *Oliver!*, *Spartacus* and *The Battle Of The Bulge*. That was the first stereo film I ever saw. We sat there and heard the planes coming over our heads and then saw them on the screen. We thought that was wonderful. I saw *Ben-Hur* at the ABC in stereo and we heard the galleys creaking behind us. We'd never heard anything like that before.

The Regal was taken over by Colin Dashwood, who ran it as a bingo hall. It was later taken over by Roger Reynolds, who ran it as snooker club. In 2004, the building was pulled down. Now all the old cinemas are gone or have been changed into smaller multiple screens. I still have my regular Monday night film shows in my home cinema, which I built in my back garden, and I still go to the Odeon on Riverside to see the big films, as they should be seen, on a big screen.

Images supplied by John Jarvis, unless stated otherwise.

> 66 The film that had the most showings at Holt was *Rock Around The Clock*. It had three more showings than any other film a week. 99

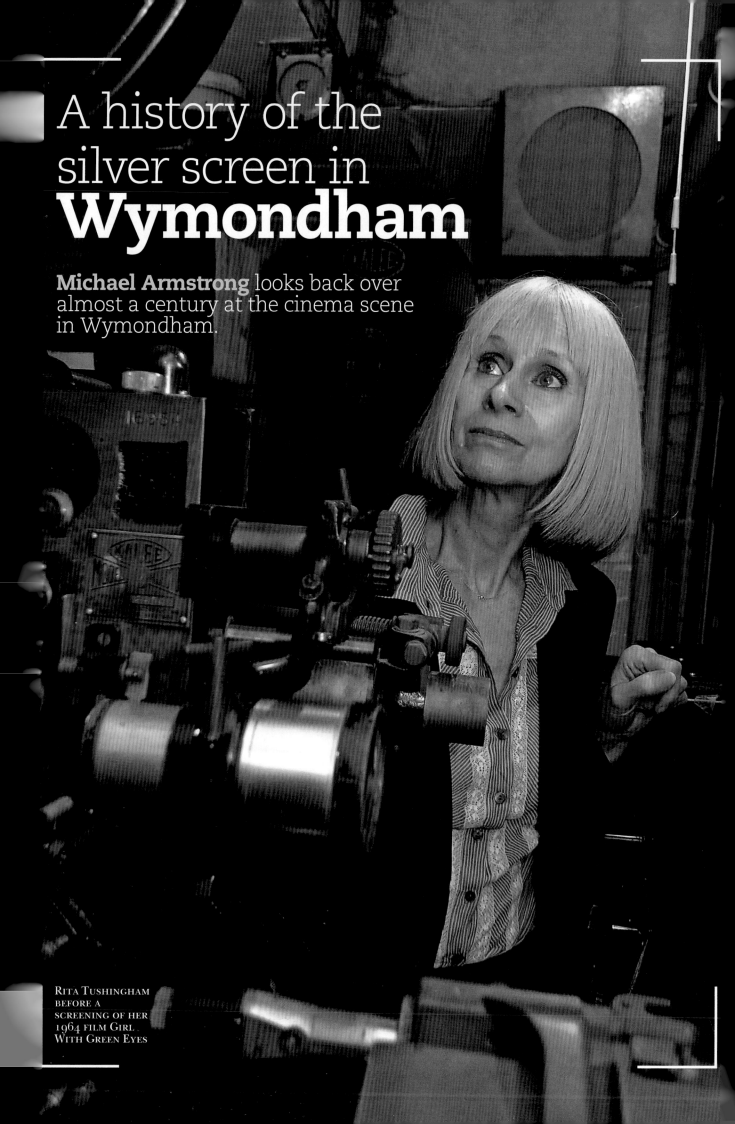

A history of the silver screen in **Wymondham**

Michael Armstrong looks back over almost a century at the cinema scene in Wymondham.

RITA TUSHINGHAM BEFORE A SCREENING OF HER 1964 FILM GIRL WITH GREEN EYES

Credit Ronald Grant Archive

SWING TIME [US 1936] GINGER ROGERS, FRED ASTAIRE

REGAL
WYMONDHAM

Phone: 149   Resident Manager: H. E. CRANE

THURSDAY, 18th MARCH, 1937
at 7-15 p.m.
GRAND OPENING PERFORMANCE
(under distinguished patronage)

The entire proceeds of Thursday's performance will be given to the
Wymondham Nursing Association

Thursday, Friday & Saturday
Ginger Rogers and Fred Astaire
in
SWING TIME

Prices of Admission:
2/-, 1/6, 1/-, 9d., 6d.
(Including Tax)   (No Tax)
(No extra for Booking)

Monday to Friday, once Nightly at 7-15
Saturday, Children's 2-30 (Half Price), 5-45, 8-15

COMING. Monday, March 22nd.
SHIRLEY TEMPLE in "POOR LITTLE RICH GIRL."

Cinema first came to Wymondham in 1917, when the public hall in Town Green started to show silent films and became known as The Picture Theatre. Residents were delighted by the new magic of the silver screen and children queued down the street to see the next exciting Pearl White episode.

The town's first purpose-built cinema arrived in 1936 when Douglas Bostock of Ipswich purchased a plot of land on Wymondham's Friarscroft Lane for the town's first luxury picture house. Bostock built and opened cinemas throughout the region during the 1930s and architect Robert Bond, who had designed other cinemas in Norwich and Norfolk, excelled in that characteristic 1930s picture-palace style, with the principal aim of providing glamour, comfort and pleasure to its patrons.

The new cinema's facade declared REGAL in neon lights. Two pairs of swing doors led into the foyer with its floor of cream and blue Italian terrazzo tiles. The curved front of the box office on the left was matched on the right by the curved wall behind the projection room (where it remains today). The auditorium's sloping floor was covered

with a thick Axminster carpet and the 503 seats had pneumatic cushion arms. The rough plaster walls of the auditorium and foyer were rose, blue and gold; the electric clock by the stage has kept good time for over 75 years, and the fireproof royal blue velvet screen curtains are still in use today too. British Talking Pictures provided two BTP projector sound-head bases with Kalee 12 projectors and Kalee Vulcan carbon arcs. They are also still in operation today.

On the evening of Thursday, March 18, 1937, there was a packed house for the cinema's gala opening. The opening film was *Swing Time*, starring Fred Astaire and Ginger Rogers.

The first manager of The Regal was Harold Crane, who in May 1937 showed free films for all the town's children in "regal" celebration of George VI's coronation. That year he started the Regal Chums Club, where children learned road safety songs and watched kids' serials.

By the end of the 30s The Regal had almost entirely eclipsed The Picture Theatre. Bostock bought the old public hall, immediately closed the cinema and sold it with a restrictive covenant that it could never be used again as a cinema or theatre.

Give Generously for your Poppy

REGAL
CINEMA - WYMONDHAM
Manager: H. E. CRANE
Phone: 149

SPECIAL
ATTRACTIONS
for
NOVEMBER, 1939

Times of Showing: Once Nightly at 7
Matinee Every Saturday 2-15
Prices of Admission:
2/-, 1/6, 1/3, 1/-, 9d. (Including Tax) & 6d.
Children's Matinees 3d.
Book your seat at the Cinema or Phone 149
2/-, 1/6 and 1/3 Bookable
Free Car Park and Cycle Store
Patrons cannot be admitted without a
Gas Mask

Golden years

The war years were the busy time for The Regal, with live variety shows on Sunday evenings to entertain the troops. Despite objection from some local churches, The Regal was granted a licence for Sunday screenings - the first was *Oh, Mr Porter!* on June 1, 1942. During 1941, chief projectionist Bert Caley took over as manager. He ran the cinema until 1962, working with his wife Dorothy, who was manageress of Bostock's Attleborough cinema, and his daughter Jean, who was usherette, and The Regal saw countless events and developments during those decades. In 1948, the foreign secretary Ernest Bevin gave a speech from the stage of The Regal as it was the only venue large enough available locally. Pathé News cameras recorded the event.

Following the introduction of the BBFC's X certificate in 1951, The Regal showed its first X-rated film, *The Moon Is Blue*, in January 1955. On November 24, 1955, Paramount's high-res, widescreen Vista Vision was introduced to Wymondham with a screening of *Three Ring Circus*. On May 20, 1957, the cinema was adapted to show its first, even wider Cinemascope film, *The Tomahawk And The Cross*. Along with trailers and Pearl & Dean adverts, Universal News was shown with each programme until it ceased in February 1959 and was replaced by Pathé Pictorial. During the 1950s, despite the appeal of VistaVision and Cinemascope, fewer and fewer people went to The Regal.

On June 9, 1962, Douglas Bostock wrote to Bert Caley to tell him that the cinema would be closing the following Sunday, June 17, after three years of running at a loss. The final film was, ironically, *For The First Time*.

Second life

The Regal stood empty for three years, but reopened on 30 April 1965 with The Beatles' film *A Hard Day's Night*. New manager Bob Harvey was also the chief projectionist. The cinema was redecorated and refurbished with seats salvaged from the Lowestoft Odeon, and the projectors were serviced.

STAFF OUTSIDE THE REGAL WYMONDHAM (MARY POPPINS)

Crowds enjoyed the biggest new releases, including the first James Bond films; Pathé News was also shown with each programme, the children's matinee was re-introduced on a Saturday afternoon and there was bingo on Monday and Friday nights. In 1969, two years after Les King became manager, a café and disco extension was built - Slade and Procol Harum were among bands who played there.

In 1973, a larger screen, taken from the recently closed Gaumont in Norwich, was installed, but by 1975 attendance was falling again, and in 1976 the cinema closed once more. Soon after, though, in January 1977, Wymondham and District Ex-Servicemen's Club bought the building, turned the disco into a bar, and leased the cinema back to Les King. He wasted no time and reopened on January 23 that year, with newer and fewer seats (to provide more legroom).

The following years were a boom-time again for The Regal, with sell-out crowds watching *Watership Down* and *Grease*, and a busy two-week run for *Gremlins* in 1984 after Les King ignored BBFC guidelines and screened the film to children under 15 (his defiance made local headlines).

Les had novel ideas to promote The Regal, one of which was when showing the film

REGAL WYMONDHAM 'Phone 3149

GRAND RE-OPENING—FRIDAY, APRIL 30th at 7 p.m.

Fri., Apr. 30 7 p.m. Sat., May 1 2 - 10.30	THE BEATLES in 'A HARD DAY'S NIGHT' — 'STOWAWAY IN THE SKY'
Sunday May 2 7 p.m.	'THE WONDERFUL COUNTRY' with PETE MURRAY in 'A TASTE OF MONEY'
Mon. - Sat. May 3-May 8 (SIX DAYS) Mon. - Fri. 7 p.m. Sat. Contin. 2 -10.30 p.m.	SEAN CONNERY, HONOR BLACKMAN in 'GOLDFINGER' also 'THE CONDORS in 'MONEY SINGS'
Sunday May 9 7 p.m.	KIERON MOORE, HAZEL COURT in 'DOCTOR BLOOD'S COFFIN' with WALTER REED in 'MACUMBA LOVE'
Mon., May 10 Tues., May 11 7 p.m.	ALBERT FINNEY, SUSANNAH YORK in 'TOM JONES' — 'WORLD OF WAX'
Wed., May 12 Thu., May 13 7 p.m.	SHIRLEY MACLAINE, JACK LEMMON in 'IRMA LA DOUCE' — 'REELS WITHIN REELS'
Fri., May 14 7 p.m. Sat., May 15 2 - 10.30	SEAN CONNERY, DANIELA BIANCHI in 'FROM RUSSIA WITH LOVE' — 'SWINGING U.K.'

> In 1969, two years after Les King became manager, a café and disco extension was built – Slade and Procol Harum were among the bands who played there.

Credit Ronald Grant Archive

Star Quality

KIA-ORA CUP SQUASH

THE REGAL SOLD THE EVER POPULAR ELDORADO ICE CREAMS, AND IN 1955 KIA-ORA FRUIT DRINKS WERE INTRODUCED.

THE REGAL HOME CINEMA A 12-SEAT PICTUREHOUSE AT MICHAEL ARMSTRONG'S HOME

Memphis Belle he arranged for a flight over the cinema of the Sally B an aircraft which had been used in the film.

In 1985 Norwich City FC won the Milk Cup, and the captain Dave Watson brought the Milk Cup to a huge night of celebration at The Regal, which had its own football team made up of staff and patrons.

During the late 1980s, however attendances once again began to fall. Les introduced wrestling at the cinema to bring in extra crowds, but The Regal finally closed on June 28, 1993, with a screening of *The Bodyguard*. The cinema was filled to capacity at a sad but regal farewell. The Ex-Servicemen's Club subsequently converted the cinema to a dance floor and bar, but retained many of the cinema's original features including the projection room and its vintage projection equipment.

The new century

Having been one of the projectionists at The Regal, I managed to rescue many of the fittings, including seats, framed stills, light fittings and the box office façade, and built a miniature Regal in my garage.

I showed films with 8mm and 16mm projectors, and when I moved to a bungalow I took the cinema with me. I continue to show old and new films in my 12-seat picture house, and have updated to a digital projector. Meanwhile, in 2000, The Regal was a cinema again for one day only, with a screening of Ealing comedy *The Titfield Thunderbolt*.

It was so popular that Philip Yaxley and myself formed The Regal Experience who, with the Ex-Servicemen's Club, arrange eight shows a year of classic films.

Stars are invited to attend as special guests at The Regal and the "mini" Regal - so far Phillip and I have hosted stars such as Jean Kent, Anne Aubrey, Virginia McKenna, Dora Bryan, Rita Tushingham, John Leyton, Shirley Anne Field, June Whitfield, Silvia Sims, Helen Fraser and Fred Astaire's daughter Ava Astaire McKenzie.

So as not to lose its former identity the Ex-Servicemen's Club have named the cinema auditorium The Regal Lounge and the Regal name will again be displayed on the front of the building.

Thanks to all those who have been involved with The Regal over the years and to the Ex Servicemen's Club for their sympathetic restoration of the building, which still provides the comfort and pleasure that Douglas Bostock established when he opened it almost 80 years ago.

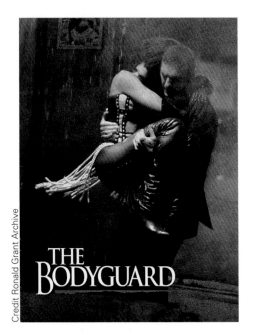

Credit Ronald Grant Archive

THE BODYGUARD

> 66 During the late 1980s, however attendances once again began to fall. Les King introduced wrestling at the cinema to bring in extra crowds, but The Regal finally closed on June 28, 1993, with a screening of *The Bodyguard.* 99

Cinema **memories**

Celebrated actor and Cinema City patron
Sir John Hurt recalls the films and cinemas
that have helped shape his life and career

Most people have a clear memory of their earliest cinema experiences. I do too, though mine weren't really that early. My parents were not at all in favour of cinema -theatre, yes - but they considered cinema a bit "common", I think.

As a child in Derbyshire I wasn't allowed to go to Saturday morning pictures or anything like that, so I wasn't introduced to all the big American films of the time. I do remember somehow managing to see Alec Guinness in David Lean's *Oliver Twist* (1948), which has a huge place in my memory. Then there was *Treasure Island* (1950), the first version that was made in colour (Technicolor). But both of those were a treat, for anything else I had to get my parents' permission, which might seem a strange concept these days. I had to

plead with them to let me see a Jerry Lewis film - I was a 12-year-old boy and he made me laugh. I thought he was hysterical. My parents just thought he was silly.

Then I moved to London and my tastes changed. When it comes to film, you could say that I'm self-educated, and that didn't really start until I discovered the films of the French nouvelle-vague.

I was at St Martins School of Art and the Royal Academy of Dramatic Art in the late

> ROBERY NEWTON IN TREASURE ISLAND

> OLIVER TWIST [BR 1948]

J. ARTHUR RANK PRESENTS

Oliver Twist

by Charles Dickens

starring ROBERT NEWTON
ALEC GUINNESS · KAY WALSH · FRANCIS L. SULLIVAN
and HENRY STEPHENSON
and introducing
JOHN HOWARD DAVIES AS OLIVER TWIST
DIRECTED BY DAVID LEAN
PRODUCED BY RONALD NEAME   Screenplay by David Lean and Stanley Haynes
A Cineguild Production

LAURENCE OLIVIER, STAR AND DIRECTOR OF HENRY V

50s and early 60s and all my friends were asking: "Have you seen the new *Truffaut*, have you seen the *Antonioni*?" I can remember all the cinemas I would go to in London; the Cameo-Polytechnic in Upper Regent St which screened all the foreign films, that's where I saw *Jules et Jim* (1962) and others. Then there was the Academy in Oxford Street, which showed *Henry V* (1944), *Richard III* (1955) and all the Bergman films. Those places are where I got my education, and not a bad education at that.

Jules et Jim had an amazing impact on me. I went back to the cinema like a pilgrim every Sunday for several weeks, until I didn't need to read the subtitles anymore. Talk about zeitgeist, it absolutely hit the pulse of everything at that time. It spoke about love in a different way: it was bohemian, it was sad, it was happy and unbelievably romantic, it was just a wonderful film with an amazing cast. That was probably the most formative film I saw - though *Oliver Twist* was on a par with that, I can remember it frame by frame.

Later on, when I first went to LA in 1978 with *Midnight Express* (1978), I remember the thrill of going to the Egyptian Theatre, which was an incredibly romantic place. Since then, I've been fortunate enough to have trodden a red carpet or two, though that has never been a motivation. I do a film if I think it's interesting.

Since I moved to Norfolk seven years ago I haven't been to the cinema as much as I

should have done but, for me, it can still be an incredibly exciting place. Maybe you don't see as many great films as in the past, the reason being that so many more are made these days, but every now and then one does come along. I saw a staggering film called *Leviathan* (2014) last year, and I thought it was absolutely blistering. It is still important to see films, where they belong, with an audience. I'm not a prophet, I can't predict where the industry is headed, but certainly venues like Cinema City are doing everything they can to keep the experience alive.

JULES ET JIM (FR 1962)

"When it comes to film, you could say that I'm self-educated, and that didn't really start until I discovered the films of the French nouvelle-vague."

The first choice for garage doors in Norfolk

Up & Over Garage Doors

Roller Garage

To arrange a free quotation, please call 01603 787069

Automated Garage Doors and Gates is a family owned company with over 20 years experience in the garage door business. We supply, install and repair a range of garage doors and gates. We are also a Garador specialist with a great choice of up & over, sectional, roller, side hung and front entrance doors.

For full details please come to our showroom:
Automated Garage Doors & Gates, Sweet Briar Ind Est, Norwich, Norfolk, NR3 2BS.

Visit our website: www.autodoorsandgates.co.uk

Pushing limits at **the seaside**

Hannah Garrard looks at the development of big screens in small towns, and how you can get away with more smut by the sea.

Credit Ronald Grant Archive

CARRY ON ABROAD
[BR 1972]

One continuous flow of mirth and merriment! That was the promise Barron's Marina Picture Palace made to the seaside crowd in Great Yarmouth when it opened its doors in 1902. Throughout much of the 20th century, the Norfolk coast guaranteed mirth and merriment to thousands of holidaymakers from all over Britain every summer, and it quickly became a thrilling arena for Britain's burgeoning cinema industry. Great Yarmouth and Gorleston opened 13 cinemas between 1902-14. Silent film stars Charlie Chaplin and Mary Pickford made their names in Britain at the seaside as well as the major cities.

The Marina ordered movies and newsreels from the French film producers Pathé, and Mr Barron accompanied silent films on the piano all day, every day - from 11am to 10pm. A huge Compton organ was the main attraction at The Regent cinema in Great Yarmouth, where audiences came to enjoy the pipes as well as the pictures. What audiences saw at the cinema was a mystery until the curtain went up; the tagline on the poster guaranteed "Interesting and instructive dramas & comedies, by world renowned Picture Play Artistes", and that was enough to draw in a crowd.

The very first moving pictures to reach the Norfolk coast were the travelling film booths at the Yarmouth fair, called bioscopes. They showed early silent-film stars such as Flora Finch and John Bunny performing late-Victorian comedy shorts. Acrobatic tumbling acts would perform on a stage in front of the screen to bring an audience together before the film started; cinema was as much a novelty as the other fairground attractions.

Over five days in 1908, around 17,000 people paid to see the first films screened at the newly opened Gem (later The Windmill). Those films included *The Suffragette's Campaign* and the intriguingly titled *Troubles In A Bathroom*, with more sober screenings such as *Incidents In The Life Of Christ* showing on Sundays. Later, The Gem promised non-stop electric vaudeville - a rolling programme of lights, music and theatrical acts. Norfolk's seaside audiences went from being ordinary spectators of cine-variety to discerning viewers of film.

The guarantee of a huge captive audience attracted the big-name stars to Norfolk. Until the middle of the century, when domestic tourism started to decline in Britain, entertainment at the seaside was a combination of live shows and cinema, programmed to meet the seasonal holiday crowd made up mostly of the middle

> 66 Over five days in 1908, around 17,000 people paid to see the first films screened at the newly opened Gem (later The Windmill). 99

classes. The Royal Aquarium in Great Yarmouth hosted big names including Lily Langtry, who came to Norfolk over the summer season to perform vaudeville. This once opulent theatre made its reputation primarily as a live entertainment venue, before switching mainly to film in the 1930s when sound arrived.

The less ambitious cinemas in smaller coastal towns also served an important community function for local residents throughout the year. The Coliseum in Gorleston opened in 1913, and could always guarantee a decent local audience, changing its film runs every three days to meet demand. The proprietor at this attractive art deco cinema welcomed audiences over a loudspeaker, and people tucked in to cream teas and cakes and enjoyed the matinee on a wet afternoon.

Going to the cinema and theatre in Great Yarmouth was an event in itself, a grand occasion where the staff wore coats and tails. People were expected to behave appropriately at the theatre and it was the proprietor's job to maintain levels of decorum. When Charlie B Cochran (who went on to become a West End impresario) was manager of The Gem, men and women had to sit on opposite sides of the auditorium - you never knew what they might get up to in the dark during saucy vaudeville routines.

The British coast has an unjust reputation of being out of step with the mainstream culture that was building in cities like London and Manchester. But Great Yarmouth's cinemas were actually able to attract major Hollywood film releases and big name stars on their first runs because of the big summer audiences that flocked to Norfolk. The smaller cinemas in

Gorleston had to wait a few weeks for the big Hollywood releases, but lagged only a short way behind their more touristy neighbours.

In the 1930s, the talkies arrived and with them came the decline of live performances across Britain; it was cheaper to show a film featuring a top star rather than stage a local performer.

But live entertainment endured on the Norfolk coast. Big film and TV stars continued to make live appearances at The Royal Aquarium and The Regent into the 1970s. George Formby and Billy Fury did seasons in the 60s, and Morecambe and Wise made appearances too. Live versions of TV sitcoms, including *On The Buses,* were filmed at The Windmill, often with guest appearances from Carry On stars. The seaside was a place of multimedia entertainment, and proprietors and managers took full advantage of the diversity that cinema spaces offered.

Keeping the whole family entertained was a programming priority: cine-variety at The Windmill and The Aquarium continued into the 50s, long after Hollywood films had taken precedent in the cities. Silent movies from the 30s gave parents a satisfying dose of nostalgia, and a rolling programme of cartoons kept the kids happy.

From the 60s, domestic holidaymakers tended to be younger and from working-class backgrounds, as those with higher disposable incomes travelled to sunnier destinations abroad. But Norfolk did not give in easily to the changing social and economic landscape, which closed many of Norfolk's best-loved theatres.

Dr Tim Snelson is lecturer in media history at the University of East Anglia, and has been researching the history of cinema-going

ABC Theatre, Great Yarmouth in 1974, previously Regal.

> "Great Yarmouth's cinemas were actually able to attract major Hollywood film releases and big name stars on their first runs because of the big summer audiences that flocked to Norfolk."

I've Gotta Horse [BR 1966] [L-R] Billy Fury, John Stokes, Amanda Barrie, Dec Cluskey, Con Cluskey

during the post-war years in Norfolk seaside towns because it has changed so distinctly. In a forthcoming BFI book, *Cinema Beyond The City*, Tim has written a chapter that looks in depth at the major changes to seaside cinema in Norfolk. He found that a couple of cinemas in Great Yarmouth altered their programming strategies drastically to keep the fluctuating audiences of tourists, locals, families and young adults happy.

"The Empire and The Windmill (owned by the Jay family since 1938) were working as a mini-conglomerate that could shift stuff across," explains Tim. "The Windmill having more family stuff on and The Empire having a more adult audience, which would shift again to more family stuff during the summer season. It was a symbiotic relationship."

During the 50s, 60s and 70s The Empire cinema screened family-friendly films during the high summer season - Hollywood westerns, colonial melodramas and Disney cartoons. When tourists went home, The Empire became a homage to horror. The proprietors screened B-movie exploitation films, and X certificates such as *Corridors Of Blood* (1958) and *The Two Faces Of Dr Jekyll* (1960) for local cinemagoers seeking something gorier than *Bambi*. This was a regular programming pattern at The Empire during the postwar years, right up until it closed in the 1970s.

As well as prolonging the life of the cinema industry in Norfolk, shrewd programming involved pushing the limits of what might have been thought decent to show in a public cinema. "What's interesting about these venues is how eclectic they are," says Tim. "Across the week they will adapt the content and material, even some more strange screenings, ones that you wouldn't expect such as Japanese sci-fi and soft porn."

Was it that you could get away with testing the boundaries of decency more easily at the seaside?

Nostalgia played a key role in programming too. "When cinemas are being old-fashioned they're doing that for a purpose," Tim says. "They're trying to attract an older audience, retired people who want to see old films from their youth, Laurel and Hardy and old Disney. That's not out-of-touch, that's playing to an audience's needs."

Seaside cinema programming was about switching tactics - knowing who was in town and what would pull them inside. This could mean *Jason And The Argonauts* in July and *Confessions Of A Psycho Cat* in October. This put Norfolk cinema enthusiasts at a distinct advantage over some urban audiences, as they had access to obscure and rare films that

city cinemas would never show. "Perhaps that's because seaside cinemas are away from the watchful eye," says Tim. "They've got more freedom and licence to test those boundaries."

Great Yarmouth and Gorleston have bowed to the rise of the multiplex, and now so have Hollywood and Odeon cinemas. As TV screens get wider and digital technology enables access to more films than we could ever watch, cinema audiences get smaller.

What will it take to revive seaside cinema entertainment in Norfolk? Perhaps the time is right for a true renaissance of classic and cult film, silent comedy and grind-house double bills. The future, perhaps, is retro.

Cinema Beyond The City: Smalltown And Rural Film Culture In Europe, edited by Judith Thissen and Clemens Zimmermann, is out in 2016.

> **"Seaside cinema programming was about switching tactics – knowing who was in town and what would pull them inside."**

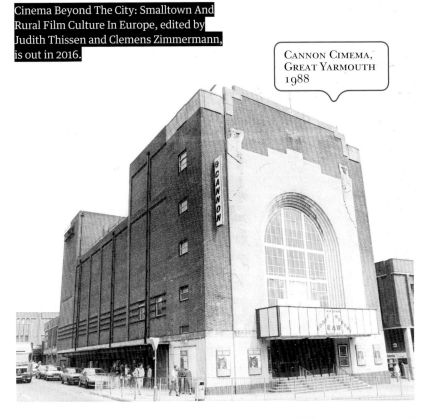

CANNON CIMEMA, GREAT YARMOUTH 1988

Cinema memories
Dereham

Colin Aldis manager of the Exchange Cinema in Dereham for almost 30 years, looks back at his lifelong love of film in conversation with Mike Hutchinson.

Photos: Ronald Newell

Colin Aldis leased the Exchange Cinema from 1965-92, but his love of the cinema started much earlier. "The first film I ever went to see was a Shirley Temple film (*Bright Eyes*, in 1934) when I was five years old," he says. "I'm sure I looked at the screen some of the time, but I was much more interested in the beam of light.

"Then my father used to work for the Shell and BP oil company, and one night a young chap who worked with him brought a hand-cranked projector to our house. Ever since then, I was very interested in the cinema."

The Exchange cinema was opened in the old Corn Exchange in 1926. At the time, there was one other dedicated cinema in the town, the Dereham and District Picture Palace, which was established in 1915. In the 1940s, it was nicknamed "the Pool cinema", because it showed films in the winter and was a swimming pool in the summer, later it changed its name again to The Mayfair.

"I started helping in the projection room at The Exchange when I was 14, and when I first worked there I also used to take the newsreels from the Exchange to the Pool cinema as they were working together."

Around this time, GM Starling was running ad hoc film screenings at his tiny Tatler cinema, which was in his back garden on Dereham High Street. Colin was a projectionist there and remembers: "It was a little 20-seat cinema. Mr Starling also had a bookshop and a toyshop. He'd run the cinema since before the war, but was never allowed to charge for admission.

"It had a miniature organ, which rose from the floor, fitted with coloured lights and a model organist called Reginald Fortissimo - a reference to Reginald Forte, a well-known theatre organist of the time. Mr Starling would also make his own Dereham newsreels using his own cine equipment - I remember him covering the local 1937 coronation celebrations."

Colin later became the projectionist at the Odeon cinema in Norwich, before deciding to put on his own shows in villages around Norfolk. "I'd hire a parish hall and pay a youngster to pull around an advertising board I'd put together on old pram wheels," he says.

Colin and his wife Miriam took over the The Exchange in 1955. "I was there for 33 years. When I look back on my life I wonder how I managed it. I used to be up at three in

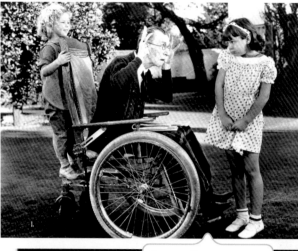

BRIGHT EYES
[US1934] SHIRLEY
TEMPLE, CHARLES
SELLON, JANE WITHERS

"The first film I ever went to see was a Shirley Temple film (*Bright Eyes*, in 1934) when I was five years old. I'm sure I looked at the screen some of the time, but I was much more interested in the beam of light."

the morning because I worked for the Dairy Crest delivering milk as well. For six or seven weeks in the summer I would also go to Duxford and run film shows with the archive there. There were a lot of mobile film units going round the villages in those days with their own 16mm equipment.

"When I was working at The Exchange, I used to order the films by ringing up London, or a company rep would come round and take your order. When you got a good film, like say *The Sound of Music*, you had to take other films as well which perhaps were not so good. *The Sound of Music*, we had for a month. When we first started off, the seats were around three shillings and five shillings. When the bingo came in they put a false ceiling in so it was bingo underneath and cinema on top.

"In the interval the audience would chuck all their old drinks cans down the front and they would land on the folks playing bingo below. That was some of the only trouble we had. Then when *Rock Around The Clock* was screening, the audience was in the gangways jumping about. We had drapes down the walls and some new seats and there were four or five boys who slashed them all along the top. The same group turned up to watch *Soldier Blue* and I didn't let them in. I said: 'When you pay me the money back for the damage you can come back in.'

"We stopped running the cinema at The Exchange when they decided to bring the bingo back upstairs. We moved the projectors, took the screen down and set up in the Memorial Hall."

NOVEMBER

SUNDAY, 3rd for 2 days
Kenneth Williams, Charles Hawtrey, Joan Sims
FOLLOW THAT CAMEL (A)
ALSO
Nigel Green, Mary Badham, Pat Cardi
LET'S KILL UNCLE (a)

TUESDAY, 5th for 2 days
Charlton Heston, Rex Harrison, Diane Cilento
The Agony & The Ecstasy (U)
in Technicolor
ALSO FULL SUPPORTING PROGRAMME

THURSDAY, 7th for 3 days
James Coburn, Camilla Sparv, Aldo Ray
Dead Heat on a Merry-Go-Round (A)
in Technicolor
ALSO
Larry Parks, Ellen Drew THE SWORDSMAN (A)

SUNDAY, 10th for 2 days
John Richardson, Olinka Berova, Edward Judd
The Vengeance of She (A)
in Technicolor
ALSO FULL SUPPORTING PROGRAMME

TUESDAY, 12th for 2 days
Robert Mitchum, Marilyn Monroe
RIVER OF NO RETURN (U)
in Technicolor
ALSO FULL SUPPORTING PROGRAMME

THURSDAY, 14th for 3 days
James Coburn, Lee J. Cobb, Gila Golan
Our Man Flint (A)
in Technicolor
ALSO FULL SUPPORTING PROGRAMME

SUNDAY, 17th for 4 days
George Peppard, James Mason, Ursula Andress
The Blue Max (A)
in Technicolor
ALSO FULL SUPPORTING PROGRAMME

THURSDAY, 21st for 3 days
Gordon Scott, Joseph Cotten, James Mitchum
THE TRAMPLERS (A)
in Technicolor
ALSO
Gary Cooper, Thomas Mitchell, Lloyd Bridges
HIGH NOON

> 66 When you got a good film, like say *The Sound of Music*, you had to take other films as well which perhaps were not so good. 99

Not content with running just one cinema, for a few years in the 1980s Colin set up his own cinema in his back-garden. From the outside the cinema looked like a normal garage, but inside Colin had installed plush floor-to-ceiling curtains, 30 red cinema seats, a 14ft Cinemascope screen and two projectors, salvaged from an old cinema.

As with many early projectors, the light was provided by burning carbon rods. Miriam and their daughter Belinda helped run the cinema, selling tickets and serving ice cream, and the venue became part of the community.

Meanwhile, Colin and Miriam had returned from the Memorial Hall to The Exchange in 1976 and ran it as a cinema again, until it was taken over by Trevor Wicks and became part of the Hollywood cinema chain in 1992. Colin recalls: "From the day I came out I didn't want to go back in, after all the years I had worked there."

Cinema City
a history and a future

David Standen looks at 50 years of the Norfolk and Norwich Film Theatre, now known as Cinema City.

The word "heritage" probably conjures up images of the past painstakingly preserved by men and women wearing National Trust fleeces. But heritage is a living thing - the part of the past that travels with us and grows as it's taken up by generation after generation. Cinema City - originally The Norfolk & Norwich Film Theatre (NNFT) - is an embodiment of this kind of heritage, connecting cinematic culture with communities around Norfolk since 1966.

Established as part of the British Film Institute's push to set up a chain of regional film theatres modelled on London's National Film Theatre, the NNFT was the first regional film theatre to receive financial backing from a local council, providing a platform for specialist cinema and encouraging learning, debate and creativity among filmgoers.

In the beginning, films were shown for one week a month at the Assembly House's Noverre Cinema, with the first programme devoted to French films including *Le Bonheur* and *Une Femme Mariée*, introduced

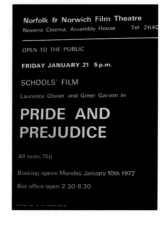

NOVERRE CINEMA MANAGER

> **"** Opening with room for 171 filmgoers to watch in comfort downstairs and 59 aloft, Cinema City was an instant hit.**"**

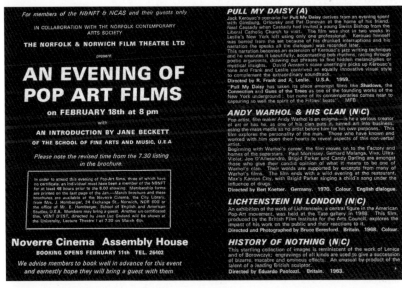

on the launch night by Sunday Times film critic Dilys Powell. The NNFT's operations soon expanded to include weekly films at the University of East Anglia and special fortnightly documentary screenings at the central library. During this time, NNFT membership swelled and, though some found the films on show challenging (including Mr FJ Wright, who wrote to the local papers to complain that *Le Bonheur* featured "as near a portrayal of sexual intercourse as, I imagine, any film would be allowed to reach without police action being taken"), thousands gladly embraced the opportunity to engage with the best in classic, alternative and foreign cinema.

For the NNFT, the "logical progression" (as it was described by then chairman Dick

Catt) from this early success was to open a "full-time cinema in premises of our own". This happened in April 1978 when Cinema City opened in the old Stuart & Suckling Halls. But Cinema City was intended to be 'more than just a cinema': it would also offer a 'workshop for film-makers in the region' and an exhibition space. Cinema City also helped the NNFT get more involved with film courses in schools and colleges, and circulate its First Cut newsletter to members.

Cinema City built on the NNFT's foundations of community engagement and education. It was this philosophy that made Cinema City a perfect tenant for its new home - Suckling House and Stuart Hall. Ethel Mary and Helen Caroline Colman donated the buildings to the city in 1925 to be used for "the advancement of education in its widest and most comprehensive sense". The culmination of a £33,000 project to convert the building into an independent cinema, Cinema City's participatory approach, with its open days, local archive film events and filmmaking workshops, meant that it could fulfil the Colman sisters' educational remit and also provide a cinema for Norwich.

Opening with "room for 171 filmgoers to watch in comfort downstairs and 59 aloft", Cinema City was an instant hit. The first programme was described in one review as "glittering", while Jacques Tati's *Mr Hulot's Holiday* was "so popular that people had to be turned away". As well as proving that there was an appetite for specialist film in Norwich, Cinema City also showed films which many people would never see otherwise, including productions by local film-makers, weekends dedicated to films made by women and a Gay Film Festival in 1981. In the words of Peter Broughan, Cinema City's first administrator: "If the shackles of box-office considerations are never entirely absent, then they are certainly less chafing in our case."

Cinema City and the NNFT continued throughout the 1980s and 90s, riding the waves of fortune as the cinema grew. The competition from the increasing popularity of home video meant there was also a renewed emphasis on the event of cinema-going during this period, with special themed showings of classic films held so that fans and newcomers could enjoy them in their full glory. This included everything from cosplaying Trekkies gathering to enjoy *Star Trek: The Motion Picture* to nostalgia-infused screenings of old British classics

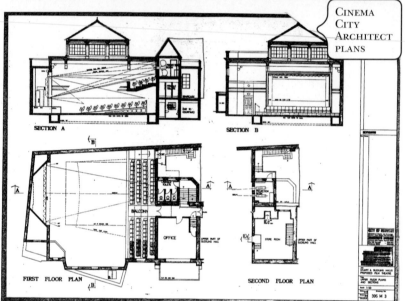

CINEMA CITY ARCHITECT PLANS

SECTION A   SECTION B

FIRST FLOOR PLAN   SECOND FLOOR PLAN

❝More still is planned, including a new specialist screening space, an exhibition on Norfolk's cinema history and an educational centre as part of the current Heritage Lottery-funded project.❞

such as the 1994 screening of *Brief Encounter* complete with original newsreel, advertising and rationing information, for which audience members were encouraged to dress up in "trenchcoats, trilbys, sharp suits and frocks of the time".

On the surface a screening of *Star Trek: The Motion Picture* may not seem to have much in common with Cinema City's more experimental offerings - like the 1980 programme of avant-garde films described as "likely to appeal only to those with a specialist interest" - but they are both examples of how Cinema City brings like-minded people together to share and discuss their love of cinema, creating a cinematic community in the process.

In 2004, Cinema City was temporarily

CINEMA
CITY
SCREEN 1

BRIEF ENCOUNTER
[BR 1946] TREVOR
HOWARD, CELIA
JOHNSON

moved to the Norwich Playhouse while an extensive revamp was undertaken. It reopened in 2007 with three screens powered by a new digital projection system.

This has made sure that Cinema City remains a vital part of Norwich's cultural landscape. As well as continuing to provide a platform for alternative and classic cinema, including film programmes curated in co-ordination with local organisations like the UEA and live event streaming, Cinema Plus has allowed the cinema to expand its educational activities. More still is planned, including a new specialist screening space, an exhibition on Norfolk's cinema history and an educational centre as part of the current Heritage Lottery-funded project.

These improvements will help Cinema City in its work to support the love, exploration and study of cinema. It will also help to preserve local cinema history for future generations, ensuring an active film community in the region for decades to come. At a time when funding for the arts is increasingly at risk, opportunities to engage with our living cinema heritage, like Norfolk at the Pictures, are particularly valuable.

Cinema
memories

Prof Charles Barr looks back on a childhood of old newsreels and an adulthood of children's shows in Norwich.

I saw my first films not long after the war at the Chandos Cinema in Buckingham. It was at the other end of the road from the house where I was born, on Chandos Road. My parents sometimes hired a babysitter and went to the 8pm show, but for the occasional family treat it had to be the first house at 5.30pm, which still meant an excitingly late bedtime.

Being middle-class, we sat in the balcony, as Trevor Howard and Celia Johnson had done not long before in the cinema scenes of *Brief Encounter*. My main memory is of the thrill of the newsreels, brief sporting highlights especially, even though by the time they reached Buckingham they were two or three weeks old. The Chandos is long since closed, and in 2014 it was demolished, replaced by a Sainsbury's.

By the time my own children were ready to see films, in the late 70s, we had just moved to Norwich. It became a cherished routine to go to the children's show on Saturday afternoons at the Noverre Cinema, within the Assembly House building.

The place and the programme had a seductive period feel, like the Chandos of old. (I recall that for a time the Noverre also ran an "art cinema" programme, in advance of the opening of Cinema City; it too has long since closed, though happily it has escaped demolition.)

The main children's feature was often animal-centred, generally quite recent, sometimes foreign and dubbed, but what we, or at least I, liked best was the regular half-hour instalment of a Famous Five-style British serial from the 50s, in scratchy black and white, featuring a child star or two, such as the David Hemmings who had

by then grown up to star in *Blow Up*.

Years later my novelist daughter wrote a lovely, nostalgic essay for The Guardian about her memory of those shows, mentioning that her father used them to catch up on his sleep: well, I might have nodded off briefly now and then, but surely not during the serial.

Now she in turn, living in Cornwall, has children, but no Chandos and no Noverre to take them to. Of course, she nurtures their cinematic taste via DVDs and downloads and the occasional multiplex treat, but all power to any scheme that restores to them and their generation the joy of old-fashioned picture-going.

Professor Charles Barr helped to found the Film Department at the University of East Anglia in the late 1970s. He has worked in St Louis and in Ireland, and is currently a Professorial Research Fellow at St Mary's University, Twickenham. His expertise includes British cinema and the films of Alfred Hitchcock.

> **❝ My main memory is of the thrill of the newsreels, brief sporting highlights especially, even though by the time they reached Buckingham they were two or three weeks old. ❞**

Thetford Palace Saturday morning

The *Jungle Book* is our first:

three of us squished together
on the double love seats at the back
that smell of coach-trips, smoke and tramps.

Samantha with her frizz of hair
and Deborah her big sister –
the one in charge because she's *old enough*.

The darkness yawns with danger
under a thick fog of smoke,
the boys in front rustle and jostle,

spit popcorn like bullets,
put their plimsolled feet
on the backs of the seats in front.

Deborah is on the look-out for older boys
but me and Samantha hold hands
on the back seats, sucking the chocolate

off of hard toffee hearts.
We become Mowgli
and Baloo is singing just for us.

Julia Webb

The old cinema is no empty bingo hall

My grandfather is a silent orchestra
towards the wind-up mirror;

before a spool of ourselves
unfurls, knots of week-long
breath slip

to the evening distillery,
Lumiere's train sweats
tapestries on white of time,

dresses unsaid words
in flesh-silk allegory,
holds peach, the cold of the street.

My grandfather is a silent orchestra,
sleeps evening bodies

in the shadow of a cheek,
the nocturne of pillars
upholding men's suits,

doesn't the screen
sluice time through screens
of dried under-eyes,

the Palaces where back-
swollen morning
ravels out like fish and chips.

My grandfather is a cinema-goer
outside the bingo hall -

the cast of glass panels
in the foyer combing
passing headlights

for evening bodies now,
beneath rusting town-trees,
to be played in reflection -

he raises me up and down
in the panels and the light,

and he hums a famous score.

Leo Temple

To speak of the woe that is cinema

Julia Blanchard and her Marlboro habit
taking you to see some French film
called *Sitcom* or *Coach Trip* and you are 21
feeling like you've tapped into a world
of sensuality and exoticness
BB on a motorbike or Serge smoking
like a bastard and the cinema the cinema
the cinema either naked in bed with Wenders
and Harry Dean Stanton singing in Spanish
or in the dark of Cinema City
Norfolk transported to rural France
with mountains motorways salesman
of prosthetic limbs and you
trying to pretend to hate popcorn
and like strong coffee from Italy
that smells like a distant dream
of some adult world you longed to enter
and then she was gone back to France
and you'd sit in the cinema like a widower
feeling terribly sorry for yourself
but labelling it "existential ennui"
as that's what they did in film
(never movies) moving sadly
like the camera in *Le Mepris*
BB in the garden with the poplar
on the horizon as you dreamed
of being someone other than you
someone who could speak French
dance in the café with Anna Karina
and sing Brel through wine-stained teeth
not a lad from Kent who was in too deep

Andrew McDonnell

Better on the big screen

I was stopped short in the cathedral cloisters:
its green shade had been replaced overnight

by a hotchpotch of animal pens and bushes,
the hot hay breath of cows and horses,

a security guard appeared, as if by magic,
barking *no photos*, the second I took out my
phone.

The ground was alive with thick snakes of
cable,
giant lights like upturned buckets,

and lounging against the wall near the toilets
were two nuns smoking and laughing,

grinding the butts of their cigarettes
into the leftovers on greasy paper plates

Julia Webb

66 Walking home after *It's A Wonderful Life*, snow in huge flakes on the heads of shoppers; their bags full of Christmas.
    After *Nosferatu*, spilling shadows on the path by the Wensum; *A Field In England*, a tether at your waist all the way back to your velveteen seat; its shower of popcorn. 99

Helen Ivory

Cinema
memories

Award-winning local writer and poet
Martin Figura looks back at how cinema has
played an important part in his life.

CHILDREN BUYING
CONFECTIONERY
AT THE CINEMA
IN NORWICH ON
11TH JULY 1970

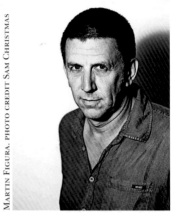

MARTIN FIGURA. PHOTO CREDIT SAM CHRISTMAS

**"The afternoon
is still my
favourite time
of day to see
films. The nicer
the day, the
greater the
pleasure – and
if it's during the
working week
all the better."**

My first
cinema
memory
is being led snivelling out of *The Longest
Day* by my mum. To make this worse, I was
spotted by classmates and my reputation as a
sensitive child and easy target was set. I was
five years old; what was my mother thinking?

In 1978, I came of age and moved to
Edinburgh, where my cinema education
properly began at the legendary Cameo
cinema on Tollcross.

It was one of the first cinemas to show
foreign films, and the queue was marshalled
by a doorman resplendent in a powder-
blue, gold-braided topcoat. After spending
my wages on books, I'd head up the

Lothian Road to the Cameo every Saturday
afternoon. On the back of *Annie Hall*'s
success, the Cameo worked through Woody
Allen's back catalogue in double bills and I
was hooked. I saw *Manhattan* three times in
its first week of release.

The afternoon is still my favourite time
of day to see films. The nicer the day, the
greater the pleasure – and if it's during the
working week all the better. I stroll past
office windows with people slogging away at
their workstations and a couple of hours later
emerge blinking back into the day and stroll
right back past them still slogging away.

This increases the enjoyment, but doesn't
make me a better person. I get over the guilt,
once a week if I can.

MANHATTAN
[US 1979]

WOODY ALLEN'S
MANHATTAN

Credit Ronald Grant Archive

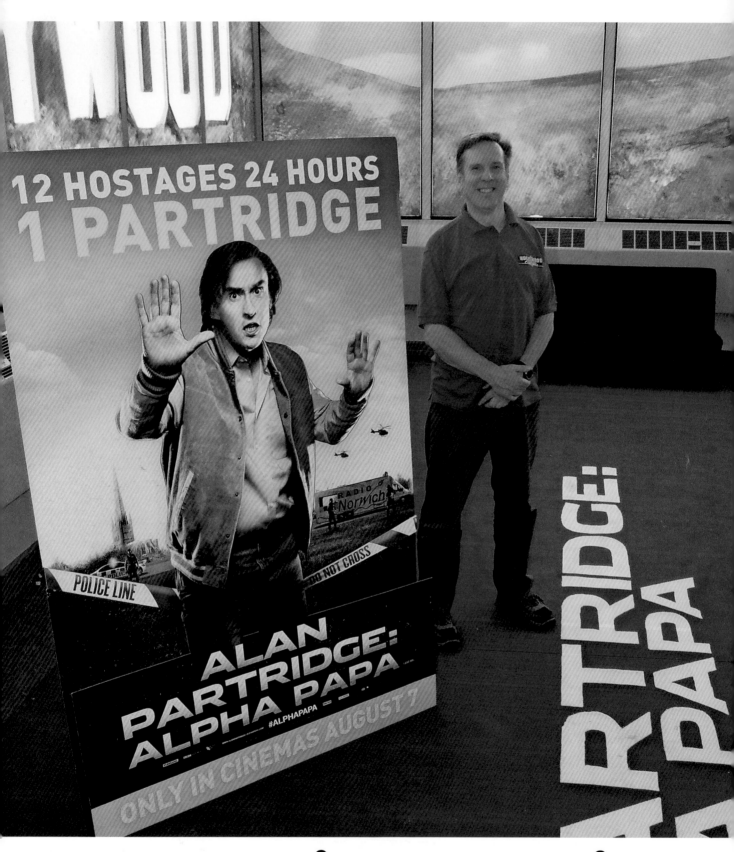

Norfolk's **mister movie**

Silvia Rose talks to an icon of Norfolk cinema, Trevor Wicks, the man behind the Hollywood Cinema chain.

STAR WARS CHARACTERS AND KIDS AT HOLLYWOOD CINEMA, ANGLIA SQUARE

A pproaching Anglia Square from Tombland, down Magdalen Street, a concrete formation looms on your left. Shops line up along the underpass, an incredibly urban landscape which seems dissonant from the more well-known side of Norwich, with its cathedrals and cobbled streets.

But if you climb up the steep steps, you will discover a true pioneer of the city's history, an establishment which has far deeper roots than the trendy cafes and barbershops. The huge graffitied face of Alan Partridge welcomes you by the entrance, cementing this branch of Hollywood Cinemas with a truly Norfolk essence.

Dubbed Norfolk's "Mr Movie", Trevor Wicks is the man behind the chain, with four cinemas under his management - in Norwich, Great Yarmouth, Dereham and Fakenham. Most of the buildings were saved from closure and kept loyal to their natural state, meaning they retain a historical character and offer a welcome antidote to the identikit larger chains.

From the first step into the foyer, I was transported back to the now closed-down cinema of my youth, The Coliseum in Porthmadog, a small seaside town in North Wales. There was the same comforting musty smell, titles of films and showing times displayed on boards with plastic letters, tiny raffle-type tickets that belong in a scrapbook. The screen rooms themselves are huge, laid out spaciously like you'd expect to see an opera.

In this age where everything is branded and systematically controlled, Hollywood Cinemas provide a lifeline back to the days where each company was a personal endeavour and staff had names and weren't just uniforms. Though the company stopped using 35mm projectors in 2013 to keep up

to date with evolving technology, there still exists an idiosyncratic character which remains defiant in the face of fluctuating trends. It's a cinema that knows what it is, and is proud of it too.

I spoke to Trevor Wicks in his office in Anglia Square to find out more about keeping independent cinemas alive.

What is your earliest cinema experience?

Probably going to see something like *Chitty Chitty Bang Bang* or *Oliver!*, round about the late sixties. I was always fascinated by the experience of going into these big buildings, the excitement of it all. I kept a diary for years of all the films I went to watch at the cinema and on television, putting summaries and stars next to them.

The first film I showed was in my garage in Necton, the village I lived in. We'd go round on our bikes telling people there was a film show on, and charge a small price for the kids. It would usually be a comedy shown on a Super 8mm projector.

Then we went up to screening films in village halls, a bit like the mobile cinemas of today.

So that's how it all started, from that little acorn. Then I had a dream that I wanted to work in a cinema. But of course, the reality doesn't always fit the dream. It's not all glamour or anything, it's a lot of paperwork, but I did all that.

When I was at school we had to do a project on cinemas, and I actually came here (the Hollywood Cinema building) to interview the old Odeon manager. At the time, I would never have dreamed that I would be sitting in this office where he was.

> " I kept a diary for years of all the films I went to watch at the cinema and on television, putting summaries and stars next to them. "

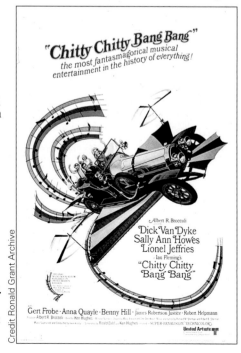

Credit Ronald Grant Archive

How did your career develop?

I began by making my own films and putting on screenings in village halls in my spare time, while doing boring jobs like working in hotels and hardware shops. But then I saw an advertisement for a trainee assistant manager at the ABC cinema in Norwich, and that's when I got into the industry professionally. I ended up in Great Yarmouth where I received my training. People seem to think that you get to watch films all the time, but running a cinema is like owning a giant sweet shop.

The films are there to draw people in so we can sell them our products. That's what keeps us going. I mean, you can love films, but sometimes the "fan" part of you gets taken away by the business side of things. That's what I found when I first started - I hated it - I nearly left after six months. But I kept at it, and found that I enjoyed the marketing aspect so I got into that. I very rarely watch films on the job, because if you're watching something in your own cinema, you're looking for all the things that could go wrong. You can't relax.

What appeals to you about re-opening and refurbishing buildings?

I love the buildings, they've got character, they've got soul, they've got years and years of people coming through their doors. Some of them date back to the 1920s. Fakenham was the biggest joy because that had been closed since 1977. It was a bingo hall that had fallen on hard times. Re-opening it as it should be - that's what I really like doing.

For me, it's important to maintain the building itself, while bearing a business model in mind. Like in Fakenham, we installed two extra screens so people had more choice. But you don't want to cram people in and spoil it, especially in a place like Fakenham where it's a listed building and still has all the gas lamps and chandeliers in the foyer... it's just fantastic.

I find old buildings fascinating. This one in Norwich is great, it won design awards in 1970 when it opened. You look at the new cinemas and, yes, they're fantastic at what they do, but there's nothing particularly pleasant about them. They all look the same. You could pick up Riverside and put it anywhere.

Do you think it's important to keep cinema alive in East Anglia?

Definitely. If I had the money I would re-open cinemas in places like Wymondham and Swaffham, all the towns that used to have cinemas. That would be great, but it's a pipe-dream.

Cinema used to be a lot more accessible. Of course, when people got cars, they could then travel. So if you lived in Swaffham, which is half an hour way, as you got older you'd want to go into the city. It's always been like that for any sort of entertainment, whether that be pubs, clubs or cinemas. So those little places couldn't have continued.

They'd cost a lot of money to convert, and in those days, the big circuit cinemas wouldn't allow the independent cinemas to show films the same time as them, it was a thing called barring clauses. The laws eventually changed, but too late for most of the small cinemas.

Has it been a struggle keeping your cinemas open? This one in Norwich for example has been open for 40 years...

We don't try and compete with the larger cinemas. We know that our audience goes from young children up to when they get their independence and want to go into the city, so we probably lose them as teenagers.

When they get older and have their own children they come back, because our prices are better, the environment's better, and our staff don't change like they do everywhere else. The last manageress who retired last December was 74, and of course at that age you see your customers grow up. Customers bring the staff presents at Christmas time. You build up that friendliness, which is something the bigger companies can't do. It's the old-school way of doing things.

> ❝ People seem to think that you get to watch films all the time, but running a cinema is like owning a giant sweet shop. ❞

Do you think cinema has a social function that goes beyond just entertainment?

Yes, not as much as it used to maybe, because people used to go two or three times a week. Now there's so much more for people to do. Most people walk around with a phone strapped to their hand, so things have changed. Everyone talked about the demise of cinema, particularly with the surge of videos in the 80s, but it didn't happen because people still wanted an evening out.

You've put on some special events over the years, most notably the premiere of *Alan Partridge: Alpha Papa* in July 2013. How was that experience?

There was a Facebook campaign and of course the Norwich connection, so we knew we had a head-start. It wouldn't be the same anywhere else. We had two to three weeks' notice to put on this world première, and it was absolutely brilliant. There were 3,000 people here, it was packed. The eyes and ears of the world were there.

It was stressful leading up to it because you think, what happens if the projector breaks down, if there's a storm and the electricity goes off, all those stupid things. But (Steve Coogan) was great, he worked the red carpet for about an hour, and everything went to perfection. You can only dream of that. It was one of those things where you wish for a Groundhog Day so you could rewind back to it.

And then last year we broke the record for longest-running film in the UK, possibly the world, which was *Despicable Me 2*. That lasted 46 weeks. It's nice to do all these things, and everyone knows about it. It's always good to keep yourself in front of the PR, unlike the bigger places where the management keeps changing and there's no

personality involved. Of course, Cinema City is different!

Do you have any future events planned?

We're looking to do a film festival in Great Yarmouth again. We've put together two very good ones. The funding ran out from the council so we had to stop them, but we're looking to do more this year or next. The sci-fi things go very well so we're planning to do another one of those. It's nice to do something a bit different, people notice you more.

What has been your proudest moment?

The *Alpha Papa* première has got to be up there. I think the big moment was when I managed to start all this, but at the time it's just a slog trying to get things going. Looking back, that would be the hardest part.

Whether I do much more, you never know. I've always got my eye on something, but sometimes you think what you've got is fine.

Die Another Day
Dir. Lee Tamahori. 2002.
Location: **Burnham Deepdale.**
Starring: **Pierce Brosnan and Halle Berry.**

Dad Savage
Dir. Betsan Morris Evans. 1998.
Locations: **Hunstanton, Wells Lifeboat Station, King's Lynn, Welney St Lawrence.** *Starring:* **Patrick Stewart.**

The Eagle Has Landed
Dir. John Sturges. 1976.
Location: **Holkham.**
Starring: **Michael Caine.**

Shakespeare In Love
Dir. John Madden. 1998.
Location: **Holkham beach.**
Starring: **Gwyneth Paltrow and Judi Dench.**

The Duchess
Dir. Saul Dibb (Ex-UEA Student). 2008.
Locations: **Holkham Hall, Cley Marshes.** *Starring:* **Keira Knightly and Ralph Fiennes.**

Dean Spanley
Dir. Toa Fraser. 2008.
Locations: **Holkham Hall, Peckover House, Wisbech, Elveden Hall, Norwich.**
Starring: **Peter O'Toole.**

The Dam Busters
Dir. Michael Anderson. 1955.
Locations: **Langham Airfield, King's Lynn.**
Starring: **Michael Redgrave.**

Glorious 39
Dir. Stephen Poliakoff. 2009.
Locations: **Little Walsingham, Salthouse and Holkham Hall.**
Starring: **Bill Nighy and Eddie Redmayne.**

Tarka The Otter
Dir. David Cobham. 1979.
Location: **Bintree Mill on the River Wensum near Fakenham.**

The Wash

Hunstanton

Heacham

Docking

Dersingham

Out Of Africa
Dir. Sydney Pollack. 1985.
Location: **Castle Rising.**
Starring: **Meryl Streep and Robert Redford.**

Sutton Bridge

Kings Lynn

Atonement
Dir. Joe Wright. 2007.
Location: **Walpole St Andrew (near King's Lynn).**
Starring: **Keira Knightly and James McAvoy.**

Revolution
Dir. Hugh Hudson. 1985.
Location: **King's Lynn.**
Starring: **Al Pacino and Donald Sutherland.**

Wisbech

Dereham

The Goob
Dir. Guy Myhill. 2014.
Locations: **Swaffham, Outwell.**

Norfolk on **screen**

Norfolk may not be considered a cinematic hotspot by most, but filmmakers have long looked to this county for filmic inspiration, says **Anna Crane**.

FILMING "THE GO BETWEEN" IN TOMBLAND NORWICH ON SEPTEMBER 6, 1970

Brandon

Eyes Wide Shut
Dir. Stanley Kubrick. 1999. *Location:* **Elveden Hall.** *Starring:* **Tom Cruise and Nicole Kidman.**
Lara Croft: Tomb Raider
Dir. Simon West. 2001. *Location:* **Elveden Hall.**
Starring: **Angelina Jolie.**

When Gwyneth Paltrow walks down the ever-stretching shore in the final scene of *Shakespeare in Love*, that's Holkham beach. The magical town seen in blockbuster hit *Stardust* was shot on Elm Hill in Norwich.

The fairytale castle in the recent adaptation *Jack the Giant Slayer* was actually Norwich Cathedral. Boasting grand halls, sweeping coasts, charming landscapes and cobbled streets, Norfolk's timeless appeal has resonated with the film industry, providing unique landscapes and settings for the silver screen.

Conspirator
Dir. Victor Saville. 1949.
Locations: **Norfolk Marshes, Cley Windmill.**
Starring: **Elizabeth Taylor and Robert Redford.**

Our Miss Fred
Dir. Bob Kellett. 1972.
Locations: **Norwich, Cromer Pier.**
Shooting Stars
Dir. Anthony Asquith. 1928.
Location: **Cromer Pier.**
In Love With Alma Cogan
Dir. Tony Britten. 2011.
Locations: **Cromer Pier, Cromer Lifeboat House, Wiveton.**

Sheringham

Cromer

Mundesley

North Walsham

The Go-Between
Dir. Joseph Losey. 1971.
Locations: **Melton Constable Hall, Hickling Broad, Thornage Village Green, Heydon, Norwich (Tombland), Thorpe Station.** *Starring*: **Julie Christie.**

The Wicked Lady
Dir. Leslie Arliss. 1945.
Location: **Blickling Hall.**
A Cock and Bull Story
Dir. Michael Winterbottom. 2005. *Locations*: **Blickling Hall, Felbrigg Hall, Gunthorpe Hall, Heydon Hall.** *Starring*: **Steve Coogan and Rob Brydon.**

Julia
Dir. Fred Zinnemann. 1977.
Location: **Winterton-On-Sea.**
Starring: **Jane Fonda and Vanessa Redgrave.**

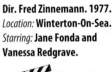

Martham

Taverham

Rackheath

Ormesby

Hellesdon

Caister on Sea

Blofield

Stardust
Dir. Matthew Vaughn. 2007.
Location: **Norwich.** *Starring*:
Clare Danes and Robert De Niro.
Cuckoo
Dir. Richard Bracewell. 2009.
Locations: **Norwich, UEA, Great Yarmouth.** *Starring*: **Richard E. Grant.**
Alan Partridge: Alpha Papa
Dir. Declan Lowney. 2013.
Locations: **Norwich, Sheringham, Cromer Pier.** *Starring*: **Steve Coogan.**
Jack The Giant Slayer
Dir. Bryan Singer. 2013.
Location: **Norwich Cathedral.**
Starring: **Nicholas Hoult.**
45 Years
Dir. Andrew Haigh. 2015.
Locations: **Bedford Street, St Benedicts Street and The Assembly House Norwich, the village of Neatishead in the Norfolk Broads.**
Tulip Fever
Dir. Justin Chadwick. 2015.
Locations: **Norwich Cathedral, Holkham.** *Starring*: **Judi Dench.**

Great Yarmouth

Full Metal Jacket
Dir. Stanley Kubrick. 1987.
Location: **Norfolk Broads.**
The Reeds
Dir. Nick Cohen. 2010.
Location: **Norfolk Broads.**

The Scouting Book For Boys
Dir. Tom Harper. 2009.
Locations: **Broadland Sands Holiday Park near Lowestoft, Holkham Bay, Trimingham, Hunstanton, Beeston Regis, Gorleston, Kessingland, Great Yarmouth.**

Beccles

Wrentham

Photo: Bill Smith

FINAL DAY OF FILMING "TULIP FEVER" AT THE NORWICH CATHEDRAL CLOISTER

Norfolk cinema
controversies

We've gone through the archives of the **Eastern Daily Press** to find local opinions and responses to some of the provocative films that changed cinema. Moving from the 1970s to the 1990s, we look at what Norfolk residents and critics thought about the challenging films of the time. **Anna Crane** reports.

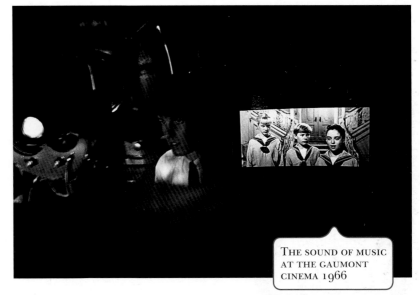

THE SOUND OF MUSIC
AT THE GAUMONT
CINEMA 1966

I t's the late 1960s and the cinematic climate is changing. While 1965's *The Sound of Music* played out its last do-re-mees, a fresh kind of edgier, riskier fare heralds a new tone for the era. From *Bonnie and Clyde* in 1967 to *Easy Rider* in 1969, controversy is moving to the heart of Hollywood.

"The last dregs of degradation have been served up to the public as entertainment," wrote Norwich citizen VJ Watt in a letter to the EDP. The cause of this passionate protest was one particular taboo-breaker which sent Norfolk audiences into a frenzy in 1973.

William Friedkin's *The Exorcist* had it all: satanic possession, graphic violence and sacrilegious imagery. The response was one of shock and disgust. "The debauchery it contained was something I could well have done without seeing," wrote one unknown local critic. The film prompted vomiting, fainting and - supposedly - emotional and psychological trauma. After searching through various medical articles on the subject, in 1974 Norwich doctor JP English claimed that consultant psychiatrists in the

city had reported outbreaks of occult activity around the Norfolk area.

"It is beyond my comprehension how anyone could want to visit a cinema where paper bags are handed round to vomit into," wrote Norfolk resident Jean M Juran. Medics were on call during viewings of the film and concerned patrons handed out leaflets outside cinemas offering helplines to call for those disturbed by what Watt described in her letter as "soul-destroying garbage". A Norwich city health committee debated a boycott of the film on the grounds of its effect on the mental and physical health of the public. The consensus? *The Exorcist* was a corruption and violation against the moral integrity of "our fine city".

But deeper exploration reveals that this response was moral panic from a small group of people rather than a widespread outrage. While Norfolk inhabitants wrote in lament of this "obscene piece of blasphemy" and called for support from those of "high morals and Christian standards", other residents were more relaxed. Norfolk local R Mellor wrote in one letter: "The non-permissive really are

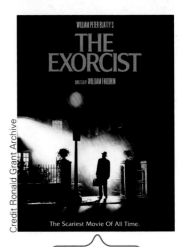

Credit Ronald Grant Archive

THE EXORCIST
[US 1973]

"Norfolk and Norwich people can draw what comfort may suit them from the fact that they seem to be more shock-proof then folks in other parts of the country."

a tiny crankish minority who richly deserve the ridicule which they go to such lengths to attract." Norfolk consultant psychologist Dr MD O'Brian observed: "It is a film which would worry susceptible people - but you cannot protect the susceptible." Another article added: "Norfolk and Norwich people can draw what comfort may suit them from the fact that they seem to be more shock-proof then folks in other parts of the country."

A confirmation of Norfolk's more open-minded approach to film comes two years later - not in the form of a demonically possessed child but a diabolical shark. Steven Spielberg's *Jaws* opened on Norfolk screens in 1975 to gargantuan success; the film ran in Norwich cinemas for 19 weeks, often playing to full houses. The critical response was a far cry from the complaints received two years earlier, though the film was just as gory as *The Exorcist*. The glaring difference was in the level of religious reference.

In 1976, another brief moral battle raged

A MARTIN SCORSESE PICTURE

THE LAST TEMPTATION OF CHRIST

> "While there is certainly a strong pious minority, the Norfolk public are revealed to be progressive, subversive and perhaps more than a little curious for the grim and the macabre."

after Danish film producer Jens Jorgen Thorsen mentioned plans to make a film based on the sex life of Jesus Christ. The agent for the North-West Norfolk Conservative Association called the proposal "the absolute limit", while Yarmouth vicar Canon Donald Holt expressed the hope that people "whether made up of Christians or not, are as much concerned with safeguarding the minds of people from false and corrupting ideas".

Another film that offered profane offence was 1988's *The Last Temptation of Christ*, from director Martin Scorsese. Cinemas in Norwich, King's Lynn and Sheringham refused to show the movie, which depicts Christ contemplating "carnal sin". Just as in 1973, helplines were set up for people to call if affected by the film. These reactions were again based on the blasphemy rather than concerns over violence in general. As King's Lynn cinema owner Tony Rowlett said: "It's been a disaster. The film has been hyped out of all proportion and it's backfired."

Flash forward to the 1990s and Norfolk's open-minded view of film is back in evidence. Just like *Jaws*, intense thriller *The Silence of the Lambs* (Jonathan Demme, 1991) proved a surprising hit for the Norfolk public. Would-be audiences at Norwich and Lowestoft cinemas had to be turned away due to the high demand for the film. "It is not often you get an 18 certificate as popular as this one," said Cromer cinema owner David High.

Similarly, Spielberg's 1993 film *Jurassic Park* had Norfolk children queuing for three hours outside the Cannon Cinema in

Norwich to see the film, despite its gore. As one young Norfolk girl declared: "I like the bit when the arm fell off."

But it was not all about lethal creatures and decapitated limbs. And soon a battle even began to uncensor rather than to censor a film: 1993 family classic *Mrs Doubtfire* was given a 12 certificate because of a scene containing mild sexual references, and disappointed Norfolk children were unable to see the comedy, which has Robin Williams dress as a female nanny in order to gain access to his children. Pioneering owner of Hollywood cinemas in Dereham and Lowestoft, Trevor Wicks, fought to reduce the rating from a 12 to a PG, allowing families and children to view the film in cinemas in Lowestoft, Bungay and Yarmouth.

So, what kind of patterns can be found in the tastes of Norfolk film audiences? While there is certainly a strong pious minority, the Norfolk public are revealed to be progressive, subversive and perhaps more than a little curious for the grim and the macabre. Particularly when it involves a killer shark or a couple of dinosaurs.

PROMOTION OF *JURASSIC PARK* AT THE CANNON IN NORWICH

Est. 1983 and run by the same family, Filby Bridge Restaurant assures the same quality & service you would expect for a fine dining experience.

We offer a fabulous a la carte menu with a superb variety of fresh fish plus an excellent lunchtime menu & superb coffee & cakes. You just need to visit us to experience great food!

www.filbybridgerestaurant.com

Filby Bridge Restaurant

2015

Broads Quality Charter

GOLD

Main Road, Filby, Gt. Yarmouth NR29 3AA
Tel: 01493 368142

Between Acle & Caister on the A1064.

f

Cinema
memories

Film-maker **Tony Britten** reflects on a
unique north Norfolk screening experience.

I moved to north Norfolk in 2000
and set up my company, Capriol
Films, in 2005. As we moved
towards production I found myself meeting
more and more people who talked knowingly
about The Balcony, or Tom and Henrietta,
or quite often just Henrietta - because it was
Henrietta Faire who did most of the work
involved in programming and accessing the
movies that were shown most Fridays at
the Faires' home cinema in Burnham Overy
Staithe.

Not for Tom and Henrietta the dubious
style statement of a data projector, wobbly
screen and tinny stereo. They had, and still
have, a huge perforated cinema screen,
proper surround-sound and an extremely
impressive 35mm projector.

As I became a regular attendee at these
marvellous screenings it became clear that,
while there might have been a certain cachet
in being a Balcony member, there was no
Norfolk snobbery involved.

The thing that unified the audience was
a love of cinema and the enjoyment of
discussing and sharing one's thoughts -
sometimes positive, sometimes not. I was
fortunate that several of my films received
a 'secret premiere' at the Balcony, although
since luminaries such as John Madden -
another local - also had sneak screenings I
know exactly where I belong in the roll of
honour!

But all good things must pass. Henrietta
found herself too busy to be an unpaid
programmer, Tom started to wonder if
the several hours it took to assemble the
authentic cinema seating were really worth it
and films stopped arriving in cans.

Not long before the digital revolution
made Tom's beloved projector (mounted
in one of the children's bedrooms!)
redundant, I went to a screening of Michael

Winterbottom's *In This World*. Michael, who
also has a house in north Norfolk, had to
cancel his appearance at the last minute
and the courier with the cans of film was
terribly late.

As I watched Tom frantically lacing up the
35mm copy as the audience became just the
teensiest bit restless, I reflected on a rather
ironic, if not downright depressing fact. *In
This World* was shot on a Sony 150 DVCam
camera - a perfectly good piece of kit that
one probably wouldn't insult a primary
school film class with now. The images were
then scanned to film and sent out by the
distributors on huge great reels of celluloid.

Five years later, they would have sent out a
Blu-Ray disc, which would have worked just
as well (the Faires had by then purchased a
digital projector). But somehow it wasn't the
same and, although Tom and Henrietta still
have the odd screening and charity concert,
the Balcony's glory days are over.

But the fact that I still occasionally meet
people who say: "Yes of course I saw your
film about Peter Warlock," fixes the Balcony
in my memory - no-one else had the guts to
screen that film!

> **The thing
> that**
> unified the
> audience was a
> love of cinema
> and the
> enjoyment of
> discussing and
> sharing one's
> thoughts –
> sometimes
> positive,
> sometimes
> not.

TONY BRITTEN
DIRECTING IN LOVE
WITH ALMA COGAN -
CROMER PIER

Location, location, **location**

Recent films *Tulip Fever* and *The Goob* demonstrate the diversity of Norfolk on screen, says Rebecca Steel.

Norfolk's eerie landscapes, unspoilt beaches and extraordinary buildings have brought film crews to the county for decades. Recent films shot here include *The Duchess*, *Glorious 39*, *Jack The Giant Slayer*, *45 Years* and, in the past couple of years, *Tulip Fever* and *The Goob*. These last two productions highlight how Norfolk locations can be used in very different ways.

Written by Tom Stoppard and directed by Justin Chadwick, *Tulip Fever* is a historical romance set in 17th-century Amsterdam, based on the novel by Deborah Moggach (who also wrote *These Foolish Things*, later adapted into *The Best Exotic Marigold Hotel*).

The story begins when artist Jan van Loos is commissioned to paint the portrait of young Sophia and her husband Cornelis. An affair between artist and model soon escalates into an escape plan - and a risky business venture. The drama unfolds amid the burgeoning tulip trade and Dutch art scene of the 1630s.

Many of the atmospheric indoor shots were filmed at Pinewood Studios, to recreate Moggach's "love-letter to Dutch painting and that lost world of serene and dreamy domestic interiors". Other scenes were shot on location across East Anglia, with the cloister of Norwich Cathedral transformed by greenery, trees, geese, pigs and cows into a lush 17th-century backdrop.

Filming also took place on the beach at Holkham, the north Norfolk coastal location that was also used in *Shakespeare in Love* (1998) and *Never Let Me Go* (2010). The cast of *Tulip Fever* is no less of a star-studded affair, with Judi Dench, Christoph Waltz and Cara Delevingne. Rising stars Alicia Vikander and Dane DeHaan play the two young lovers.

Norfolk locations are often used for stories that take place elsewhere, like Amsterdam in *Tulip Fever*, but *The Goob* is noteworthy because it's based where it's filmed - in rural Norfolk. A gritty tale in the socio-realist tradition of independent British cinema, *The Goob* draws inspiration from locations

> "
> *The Goob* draws inspiration from locations around Swaffham such as Necton Diner and the Raceway. "

PHOTO: EMU FILMS — AMELIA TROUBRIDGE

> **❝** Other scenes were shot on location across East Anglia, with the cloister of Norwich Cathedral transformed by greenery, trees, geese, pigs and cows into a lush 17th-century backdrop. **❞**

around Swaffham such as Necton Diner and the Raceway. The film centres on 16-year-old Goob, whose mother runs a transport cafe. It's the summer after he finishes school, and Goob is working as a field labourer and hanging out at the Raceway. Family tensions are running high, largely because of the bullying behaviour of his mother's cheating boyfriend.

The Goob's writer and director, Guy Myhill, was prompted to make the film after spending time at Swaffham Raceway while filming a Channel 4 documentary about stock-car racing; inspiration also came from the agricultural vistas around Necton and the transient nature of seasonal farm work.

Filmed in August 2013, *The Goob* depicts balmy summer evenings and the magical beauty of rural Norfolk. Simon Tindall's stunning cinematography shows great sensitivity towards the landscape, complemented by an award-winning electronic soundtrack from Luke Abbott.

The film sought to include Norfolk accents and benefit the Norfolk economy by using local cast and crew. First-time actor Liam Walpole landed the role of Goob after he was spotted in Dereham. Several other cast members have connections with East Anglia,

including Sienna Guillory, a former student at Gresham's School in Holt, Bafta-winner Sean Harris, who grew up in Lowestoft, and Gorleston-born Hannah Spearritt.

Films like *The Goob*, backed by Creative England's iFeatures programme, contribute a new and alternative angle to filming in the region. They also encourage and retain local talent - like that of Norwich-based director Guy Myhill. Norfolk's role in the creative industries could become even more exciting if this formula is replicated in the future.

The Goob is available on DVD from September 21, 2015. Tulip Fever is due for release in cinemas from autumn 2015. Our interview with 45 Years director Andrew Haigh is on pages 90-91.

The Goob Q&A

Writer and director **Guy Myhill** talks to Charlotte Day about shooting *The Goob* in Norfolk.

What prompted you to film *The Goob* in Norfolk?

I'd made a documentary on stock-car racing for Channel 4 at a track in Swaffham and there was a vibrancy, a sense of colour and noise that really appealed. Swaffham is in my top 10 of Norfolk locations, specifically because of the stock-car tracks. It's the visual element you're getting from that - the sound and the sense of freshness.

Was it important for you to work with Norfolk-based talent?

The actors had to have a real sense of authenticity, with their dialogue and their look. We were just so lucky with Liam (Walpole, who plays Goob). We had a group of casting people who walked round Dereham market and got permission to take a photo of anyone who looked likely. Liam wasn't in the original top 10 of candidates, but I was in such a panic with three weeks to go that I just looked through everything and his face came up. From the outset, I wanted this sense of someone who didn't really belong there but you could tell was from there. An early reference point was David Bowie in *The Man Who Fell To Earth*. When I saw Liam's picture, I knew he had that quality.

Luke Abbott composed the soundtrack. What was it about his music that was right for the film?

It comes back to authenticity. I could have just gone to an everyday film composer, and it's rare that you get an electronic score for a film, but I knew Luke's music and I wanted to see if it would work. Then when we first met he spoke about what he wanted to do in relation to *The Goob*, about expressing the landscape and about seeing these flatlands as a series of drones. It's also about using as many people as you can who have a connection with the region - Sean (Harris) is from Lowestoft, Sienna (Guillory) is from Holt and Hannah (Spearritt) is from Great Yarmouth. I've been making films with Sean for 20 years.

Can you tell us a bit more about the locations you used?

It was all shot in Norfolk; as well as the stock-car track we had Necton Diner on the way to King's Lynn which just looks great - it's low slung with a big chimney and it's got this American feel. Both these locations were key. Then we had a great place, the business name is Doubledays and they're out Wisbech way. They have migrant workers as well as English people working for them and they have a whole series of caravans and battered trailers round the back, so we used that as a backdrop along with the surrounding fields.

What future projects are you working on – and will they be set in Norfolk?

The Goob is part of a Norfolk-based trilogy, so yes! I've just put in the script to the BFI and BBC. It's based on a travelling show that starts in Coventry and ends up on the coast in Great Yarmouth. A couple of years ago I did a documentary where I lived with a circus and the seeds for it came from that. We'll probably have Sean in it again too.

GUY MYHILL, PICTURE: ANDI SAPEY

"It was all shot in Norfolk; as well as the stock-car track we had Necton Diner on the way to King's Lynn which just looks great – it's low slung with a big chimney and it's got this American feel."

Norfolk's
barren beauty

Writer and director **Andrew Haigh** made his second feature in and around the Broads and Norwich before heading stateside to San Francisco.

By Anna Blagrove

Images: Agatha A Nitecka

TRISTAN GOLIGHER AND ANDREW HAIGH SCOUT LOCATIONS IN NORWICH.

F ormer Norwich Golden Triangle resident Andrew Haigh, whose debut feature *Weekend* was a huge indie hit, now lives in California where he's made two seasons of acclaimed HBO drama *Looking*. Before he left for the US, he wrote and directed *45 Years*. Starring Charlotte Rampling and Tom Courtenay as a couple approaching their 45th wedding anniversary, the film is shot in rural Norfolk, around the broads, and in Norwich.

45 Years presents a new take on relationships in older age and succeeds in not patronising or sentimentalising the

ANDREW HAIGH WITH CHARLOTTE RAMPLING

characters. The film is compassionate, sharply observed and subtly funny, and looks in-depth at a phase of life often seen only in the background, caricatured or excluded altogether from film narratives. It also offers Rampling and Courtenay, two of the UK's finest actors their best roles in years, and confirms Haigh as a writer and director with a knack for portraying authentic characters and situations.

Tristan Goligher is *45 Years*' producer, and a producer at the dynamic British production company, The Bureau. Goligher has in fact been Exec Producer for another two films shot in Norfolk in the last few years (*The Goob* and *Norfolk*), and although he hails from Northern Ireland, has enjoyed shooting in the county. He has this to say about the area:

"Norfolk is an interesting place...there are interesting, artistic people here. The landscape is amazing. The sorts of films I'm drawn to are trying to do something a bit different and one of the biggest issues we have with British cinema is that our films are either about London or about poor people living on council estates outside London. Neither of those things particularly interest me. That is not how most people in the UK actually live. So the idea of telling stories about real people experiencing real emotions is for me much more interesting. As it turned out, three of those stories that I came across were set in this landscape."

We spoke with Andrew Haigh just before the film's release.

Why did you choose to film *45 Years* in Norfolk?

Norwich and the surrounding countryside were perfect for the story. There is a barren beauty to the open landscape that reflected the emotions within the story perfectly. I was also living in Norwich at the time so I knew the area well. I feel like it's still an undiscovered part of the country, which is just fine by me.

Which exact locations did you shoot at?

We shot throughout Norwich, in the market, at the Assembly Rooms, and in cafes across the city. We also shot in the village of Neatishead, at Cantley's sugar factory and in the surrounding countryside.

Did you employ any local cast and crew?

Wherever we could, we would hire local. A lot of the locations team, assistant directors

Tom Courtenay as Geoff Mercer, on location at The Assembly House, Norwich.

and runners came from the area. We also had a lot of background supporting actors, which was great.

What are the advantages of filming in this county? What are the drawbacks?

There are not really any disadvantages as far as I could tell other than the area is not set up for film production as such and so equipment needs to come from London, but that's not really a problem. It's only two hours away after all.

Would you film in the east of England again?

It would always depend on the story - but if the story suited it then of course.

Have you got any experience of going to the cinema in Norfolk?

I don't think I could have lived in a city that didn't have a good independent cinema and Cinema City is a great cinema with a varied and diverse programme. When *Weekend* came out I did a Q&A there and it was really fun. It was even better to be able to walk home at the end of the night.

■ *45 Years* **is on general release from August 28, 2015.**

66
I don't think I could have lived in a city that didn't have a good independent cinema and Cinema City is a great cinema with a varied and diverse programme. 99

Cinema **today**

Lifelong film-lover and film education professional **Guy Martin** looks to a rosy future for cinema.

NORWICH
RIVERSIDE
ODEON CINEMA
AT NIGHT.

Guy Martin, photo credit K.Mager

I grew up in the West Midlands and my earliest memories of the big screen were those unforgettable first trips to my local cinemas, The Central in Kidderminster and The Haven in Stourport. It was there that I saw my first James Bond film, *The Man with the Golden Gun*, as well as *Escape From The Planet Of The Apes* (on a double bill with P*lanet Of The Apes*), *At The Earth's Core, Close Encounters,* and *Star Wars*. Perhaps most vividly, I remember the excitement and terror I felt watching *Jaws*, which soon replaced the disappointment I felt that my dad and I had got the times wrong and missed the opening 10 minutes.

Then the cinemas closed. The Haven in 1976 and The Central in 1982. Both were turned into supermarkets. Apparently on the last night of The Haven, the manager, seeing only three customers had turned up, closed the doors for good and headed down the pub.

Throughout my teens, my nearest cinemas were in Birmingham and Bridgenorth, 15 or 20 miles away. Still, with my friends, I would make the trek every week in order to experience *Blade Runner, ET, Videodrome, Friday 13th 3* (in somewhat shonky 3D!), *Airplane, Ghostbusters* and I think every Steve Martin film that was released.

During this time, across the country, cinema attendances continued to plummet, hitting their lowest point in 1983 with just 54 million tickets sold. To put this in some kind

Credit Ronald Grant Archive

JAWS [US 1975]

66 Most people, me included, do largely welcome the changes. Behind the scenes though, the reality has perhaps been more contentious. As the memories and testimonies in this magazine have shown, with the demise of celluloid, many would argue we have lost a great deal, not least the craft of the projectionist. **99**

of context, in 1946 admissions had peaked at 1.64 billion. Then, in 1985, the first multiplex opened in Milton Keynes.

When I eventually moved to London, I couldn't believe there were so many cinemas to choose from - most exciting of all, the one-screen repertory cinemas where I would get to explore the best of independent, foreign and schlock cinema. The Scala at King's Cross was my favourite. I remember the legendary Scala cat, which would suddenly leap on to your lap in the darkness - not really what you wanted in the midst of a Dario Argento double-bill.

I ended up working in a cinema, of course. During the 1990s I remember, one-by-one, all the single-screen and repertory cinemas in London disappearing. The Lumière on St Martin's Lane closed in 1997. The Scala had closed its wonderful shabby doors in 1993. Meanwhile, the march of the multiplexes continued unabated.

Writing this in 2015 I'm genuinely surprised and heartened to see so many cinemas springing up, especially the many small "boutique" and rural venues. This is, of course, a lot to do with the transition to digital technologies. It also says a lot about the public's continued appetite for the communal experience of sitting together and being drawn into another world. There is another reason though. Cinemas have changed dramatically over the last decade, to the point where the whole idea of what a cinema is and what it can offer has been transformed. A glance at the programmes of Cinema City, and many other cinemas, makes this abundantly clear.

Alongside new releases, you will find live theatre and opera, satellite interviews with directors, live concerts and comedy. You can even take your baby into special morning

screenings. Traditionally, these additional programming strands might be expected to be part of the offer of independent and arthouse cinemas, but now the multiplexes are getting in on the act with VIP seating and food and drink offers. Now it's all about the experience, and it's all down to digital.

Most people, me included, do largely welcome the changes. Behind the scenes though, the reality has perhaps been more contentious. As the memories and testimonies in this magazine have shown, with the demise of celluloid, many would argue we have lost a great deal, not least the craft of the projectionist. Whereas we would previously idly imagine the projectionist carefully lacing up the feature and orchestrating the lights, now I'm afraid it is more likely to be a piece of computer software that controls the performance.

Nonetheless, the cinema industry is in a relatively robust place with annual admissions located around the 170 million mark for the past decade. Concerns have recently been raised again in the trade magazines following a dip in admissions this year and the recent flurry of enthusiasm for 3D seems to have abated (don't we ever learn?). For my own part, I place the blame at least partly with the tremendous lack of ambition being shown by the mainstream studios.

The endless conveyor belt of unremarkable CGI-heavy superhero sequels compared with the high quality of television writing at the moment is a case in point. But, if anything, the memories in this magazine surely prove that these things go in cycles.

I saw *Jaws* again a couple of years ago here at Cinema City - a newly restored digital print. It would have been as sharp and vivid as that first time I saw it at The Central in 1975 - in fact, the picture quality was probably better this time round.

And the thing is, it all came flooding back - the feeling of seeing it for the very first time in a way I'd never experienced during the countless repeat viewings on TV, or VHS or DVD. What's more, this time I made sure I got to see the whole film. And guess what? There's a cinema back in Kidderminster again.

THE JERK [US 1979]
STEVE MARTIN

Credit Ronald Grant Archive